Big Book of Patterns

Table of Contents

About This Book

Packed with loads of patterns and clip art covering a wide range of popular themes and curriculum-related topics, *Big Book of Patterns* is the perfect resource for creating an eye-catching and inviting classroom! Inside you'll find art adapted from *The Mailbox®* line of magazines and books. Use it to enhance all kinds of things:

- reproducibles, games, and centers
- awards and incentives
- nametags and labels
- bulletin boards, posters, and banners
- student work displays
- parent communications and newsletters
- and more!

All art is arranged alphabetically and grouped by theme or topic so you can quickly find the pattern or clip art suited for your individual needs. With hundreds of ready-to-use pieces of art, *Big Book of Patterns* is a tremendous timesaving resource that you can use all year long!

Managing Editor: Jennifer Munnerlyn
Editor at Large: Diane Badden
Copy Editors: Tazmen Carlisle, Amy Kirtley-Hill, Karen L. Mayworth, Kristy Parton, Debbie Shoffner, Cathy Edwards Simrell
Cover Artist: Clevell Harris
Art Coordinator: Theresa Lewis Goode
Artists: Pam Crane, Theresa Lewis Goode, Clevell Harris, Ivy L. Koonce, Sheila Krill, Clint Moore, Greg D. Rieves, Rebecca Saunders, Barry Slate, Donna K. Teal
The Mailbox® Books.com: Jennifer Tipton Bennett (DESIGNER/ARTIST); Stuart Smith (PRODUCTION ARTIST); Karen White (INTERNET COORDINATOR); Paul Fleetwood, Xiaoyun Wu (SYSTEMS)

President, The Mailbox Book Company™: Joseph C. Bucci
Director of Book Planning and Development: Chris Poindexter
Curriculum Director: Karen P. Shelton
Book Development Managers: Cayce Guiliano, Elizabeth H. Lindsay, Thad McLaurin
Editorial Planning: Kimberley Bruck (MANAGER); Debra Liverman, Sharon Murphy, Susan Walker (TEAM LEADERS)
Editorial and Freelance Management: Karen A. Brudnak; Hope Rodgers (EDITORIAL ASSISTANT)
Editorial Production: Lisa K. Pitts (TRAFFIC MANAGER); Lynette Dickerson (TYPE SYSTEMS); Mark Rainey (TYPESETTER)
Librarian: Dorothy C. McKinney

Manufactured in the United States
10 9 8 7 6 5 4 3 2 1

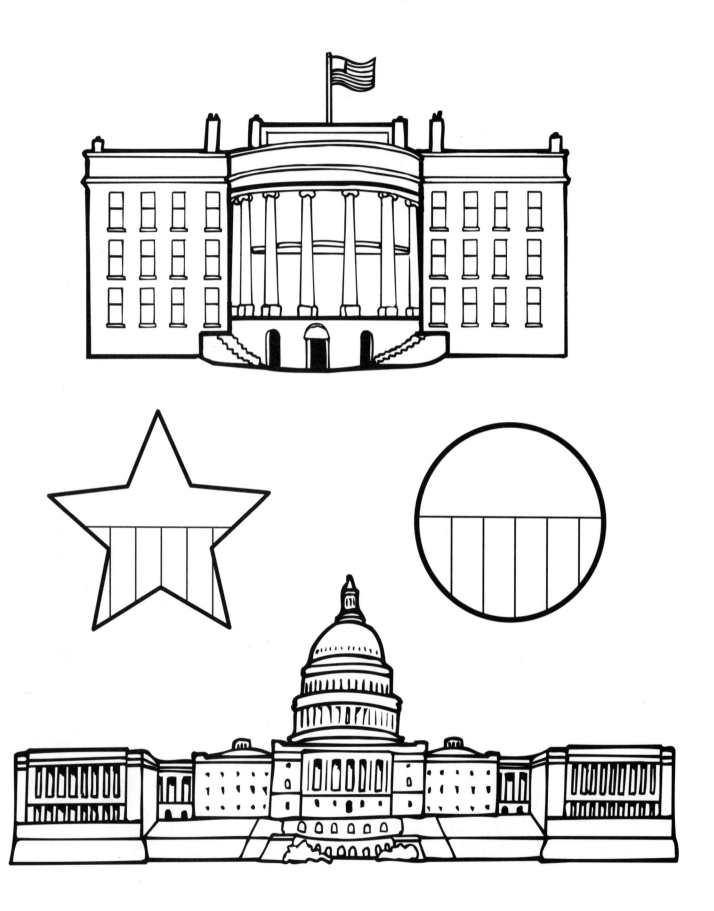

4

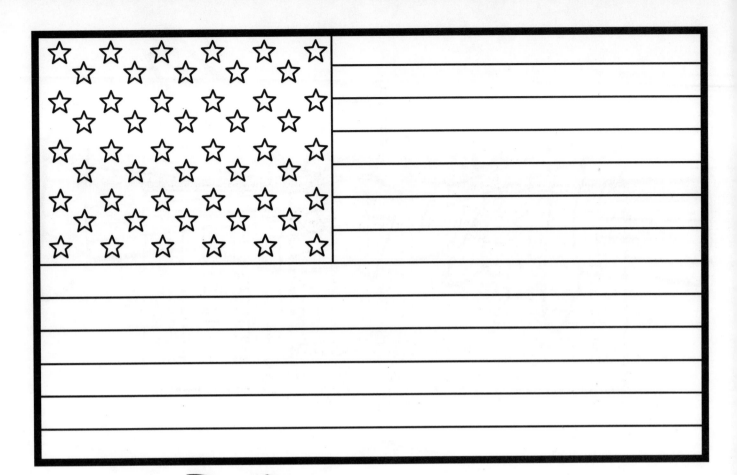

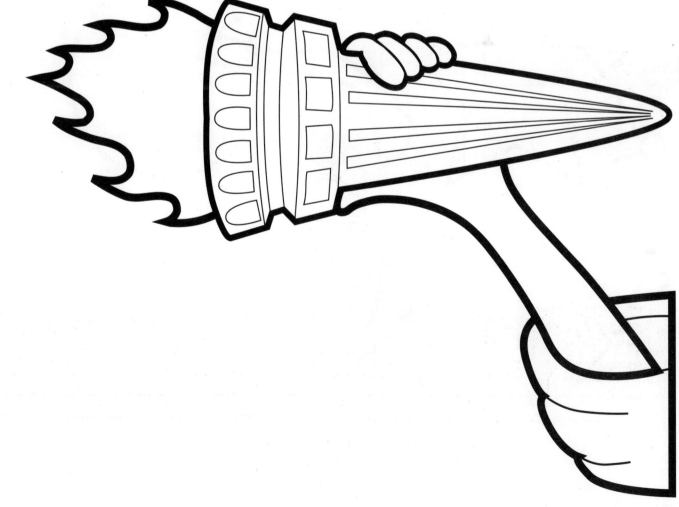

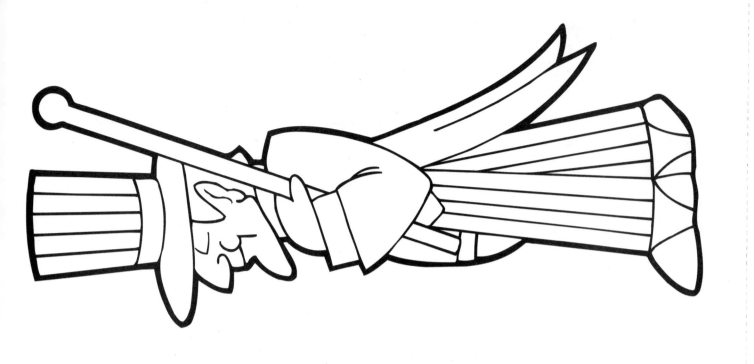

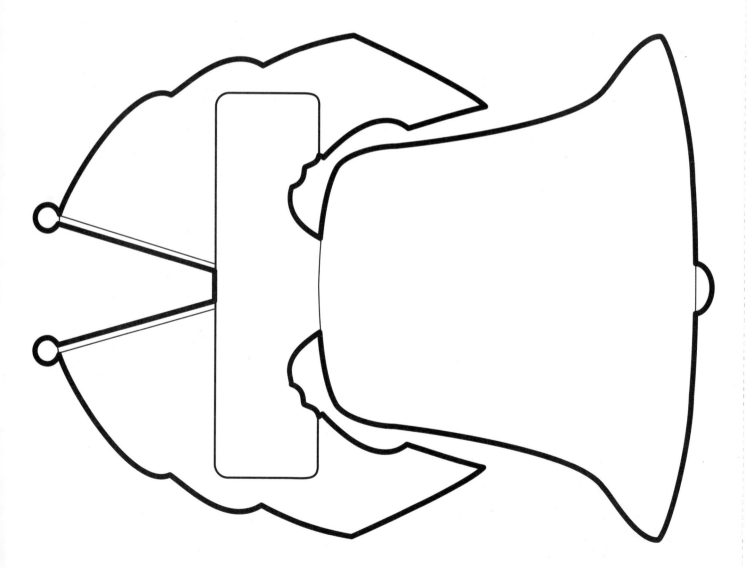

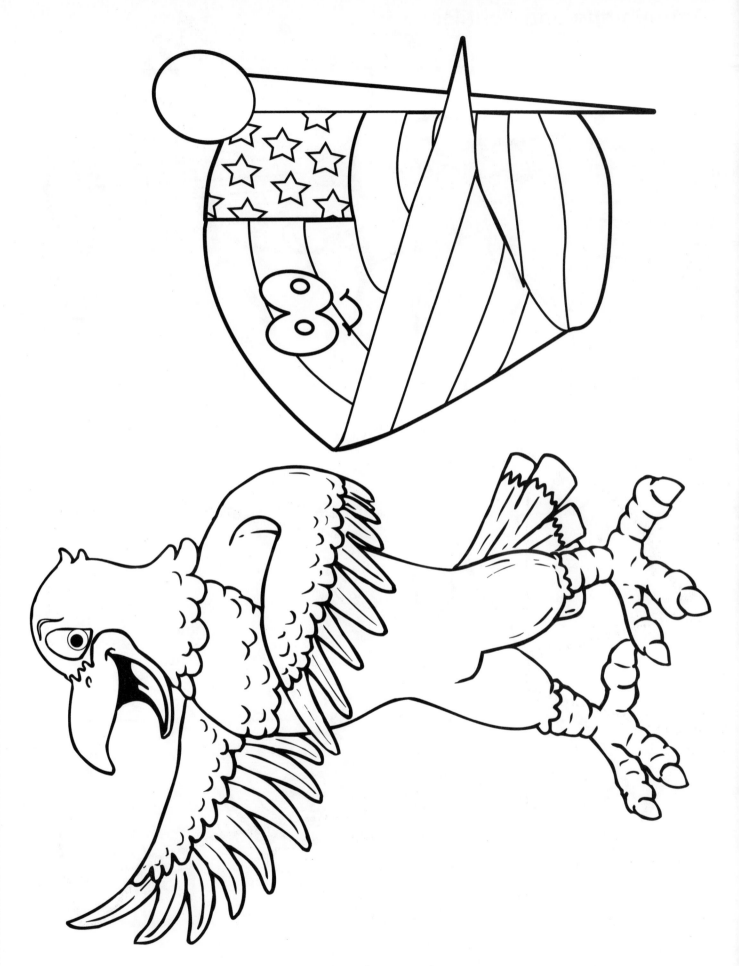

Amphibians and Reptiles

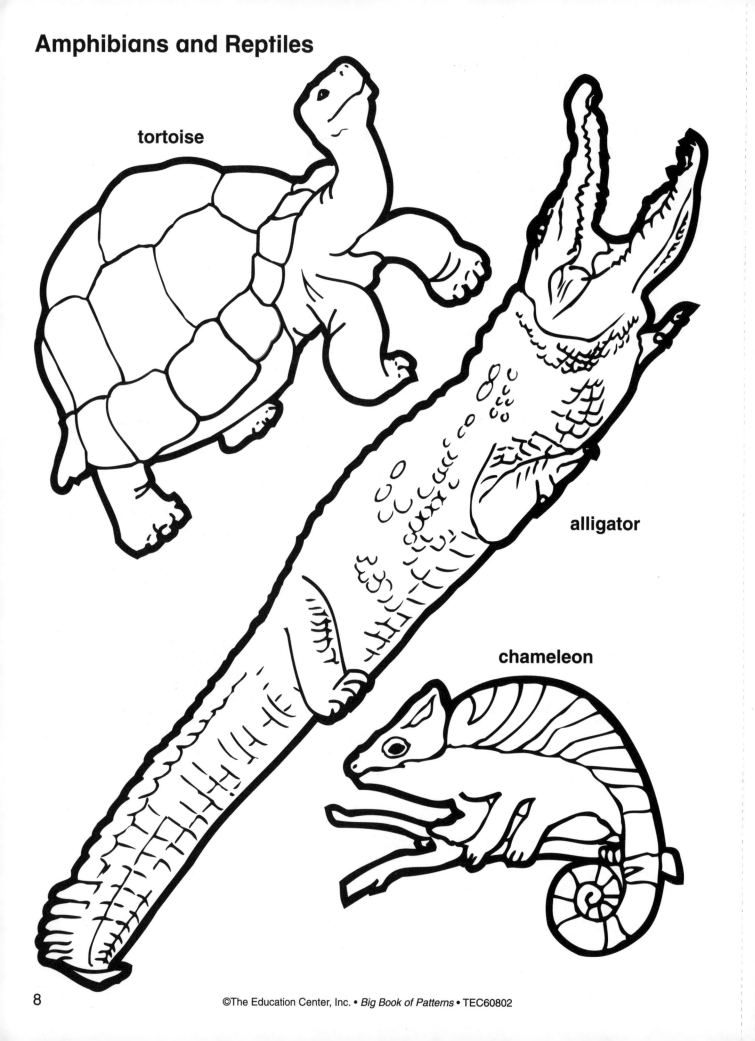

tortoise

alligator

chameleon

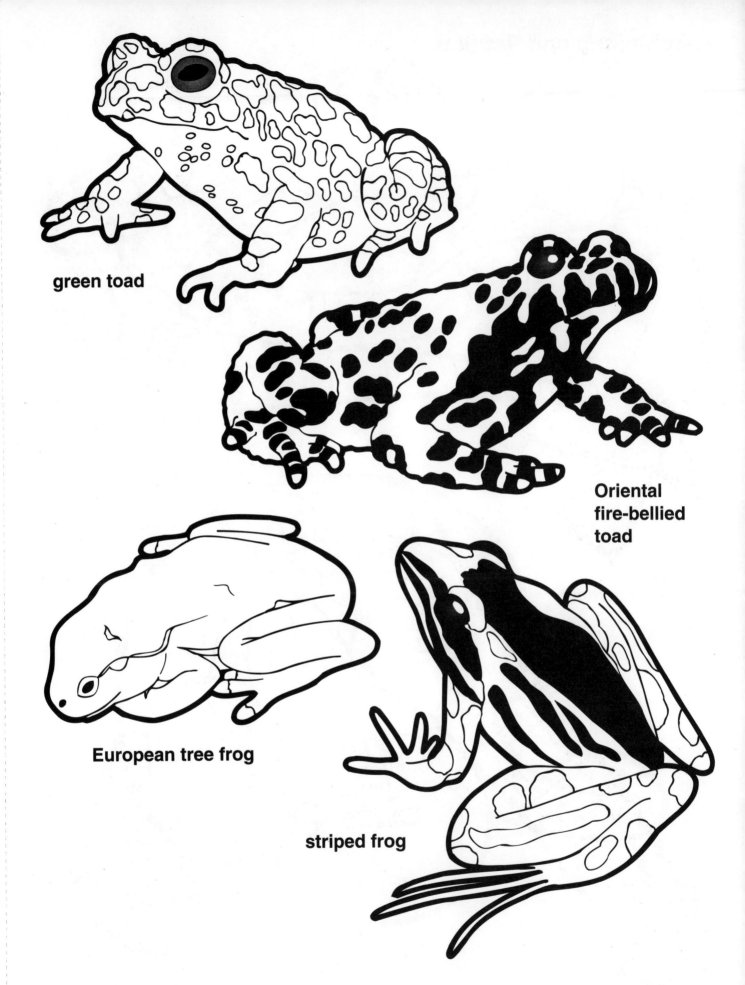

green toad

Oriental
fire-bellied
toad

European tree frog

striped frog

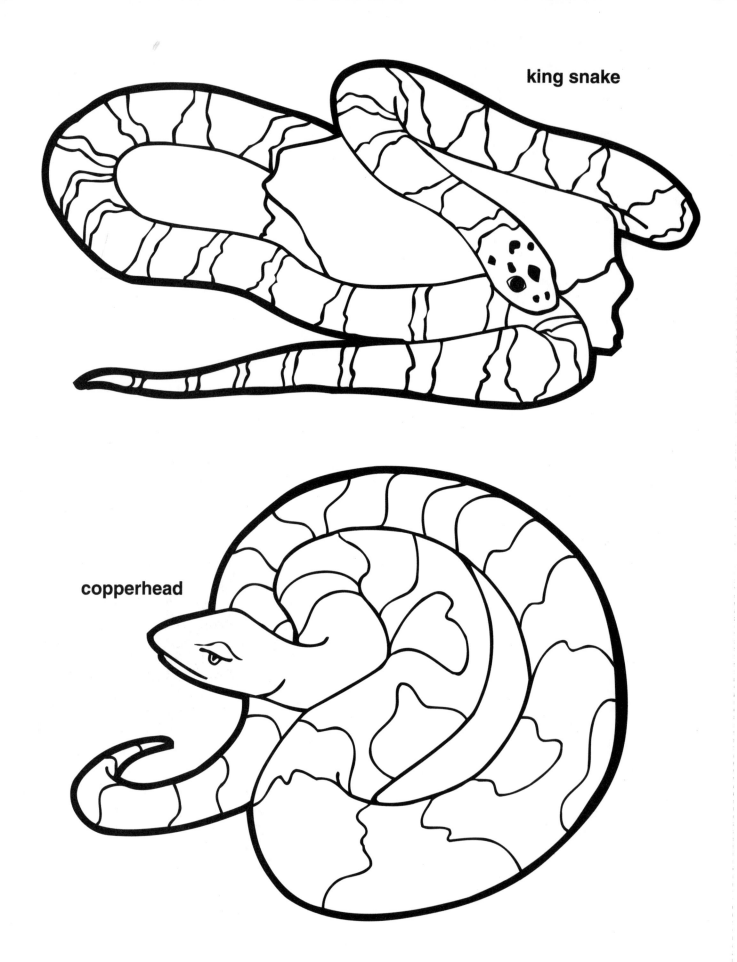

king snake

copperhead

gekko   **salamander**

PAINT

Washable Marker

COLORFUL
CRAYONS
8 LARGE CRAYONS
8 LARGE CRAYONS

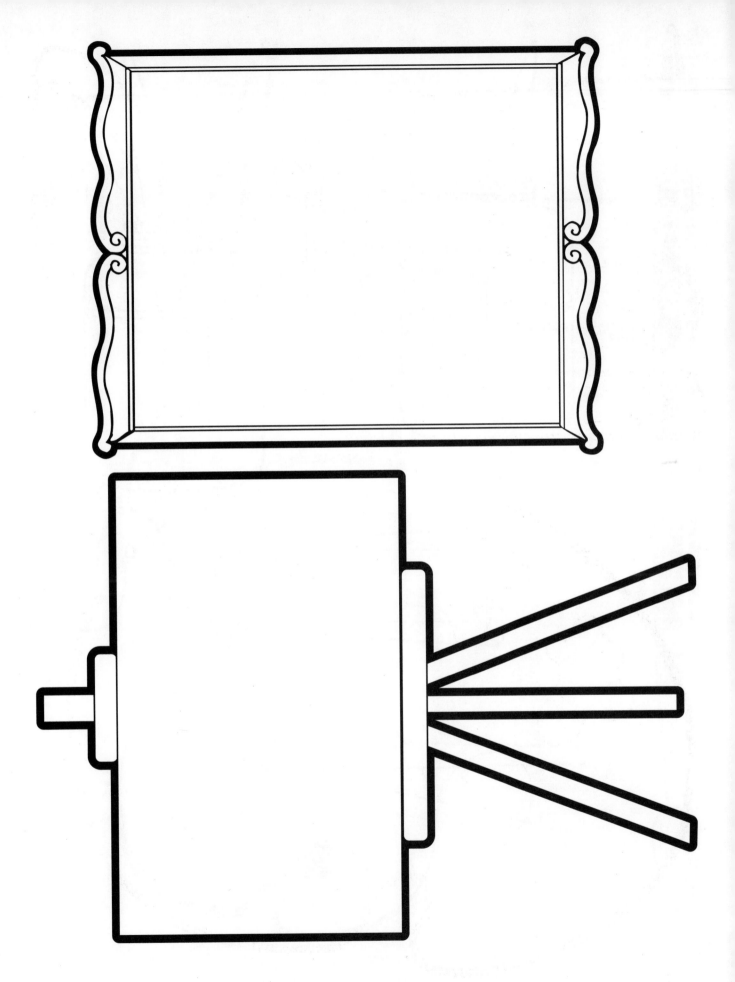

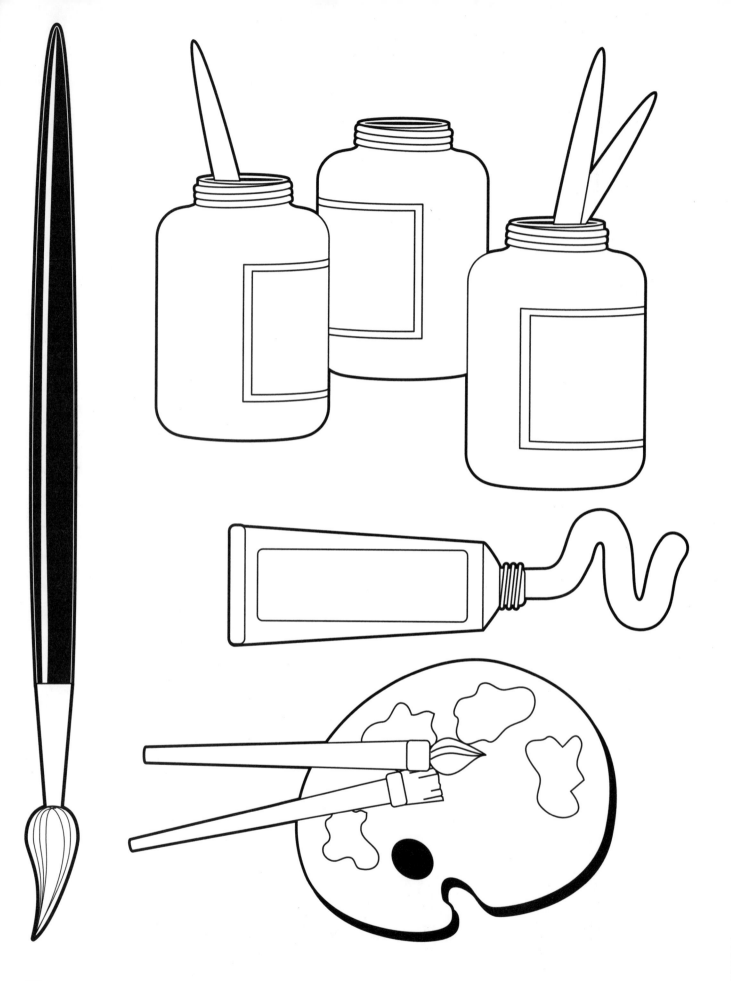

art assignment

Birds

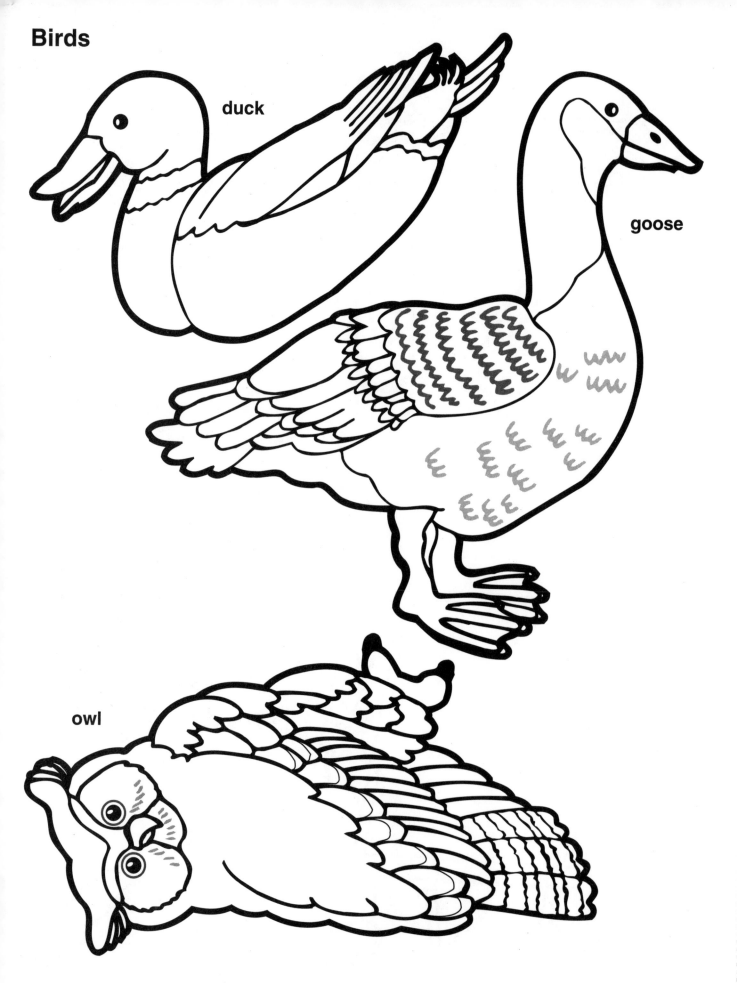

duck

goose

owl

cardinal

blue jay

penguin

ostrich

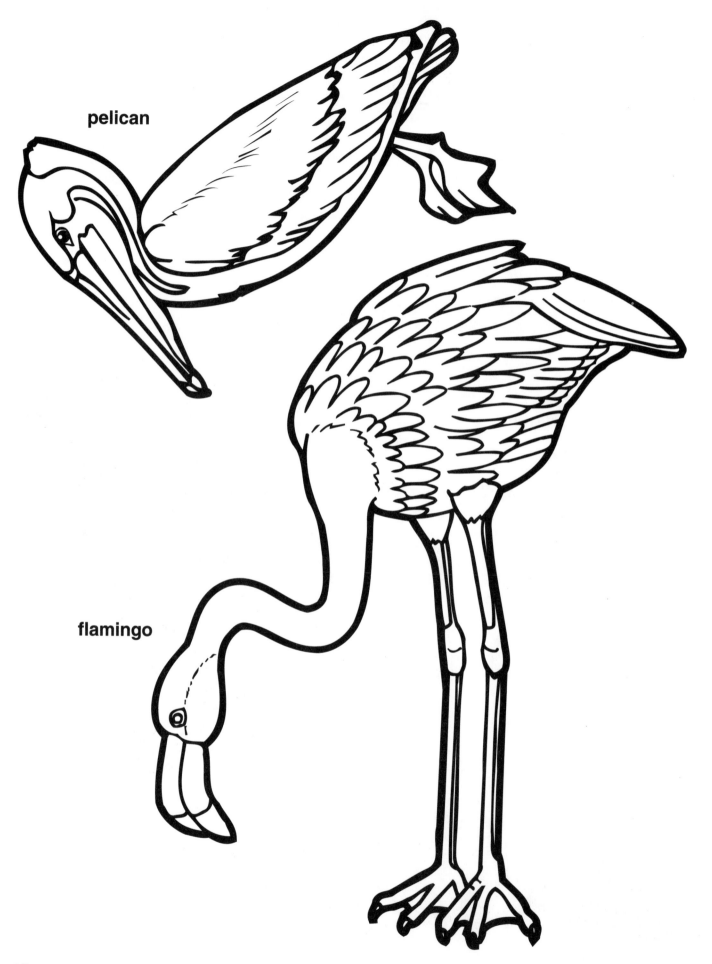

pelican

flamingo

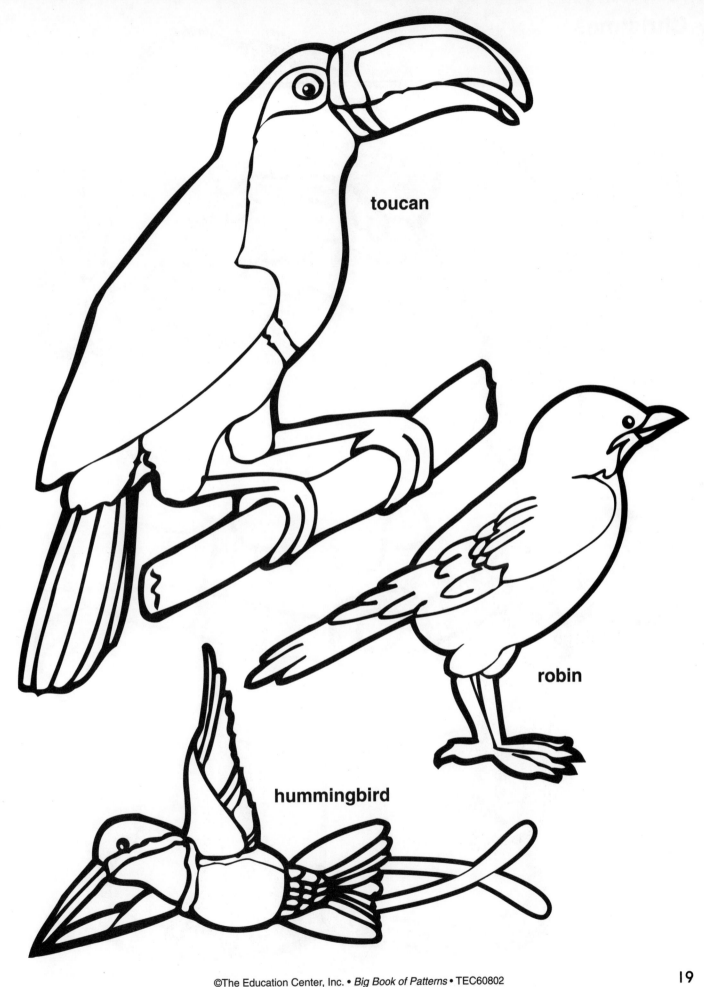

toucan

robin

hummingbird

21

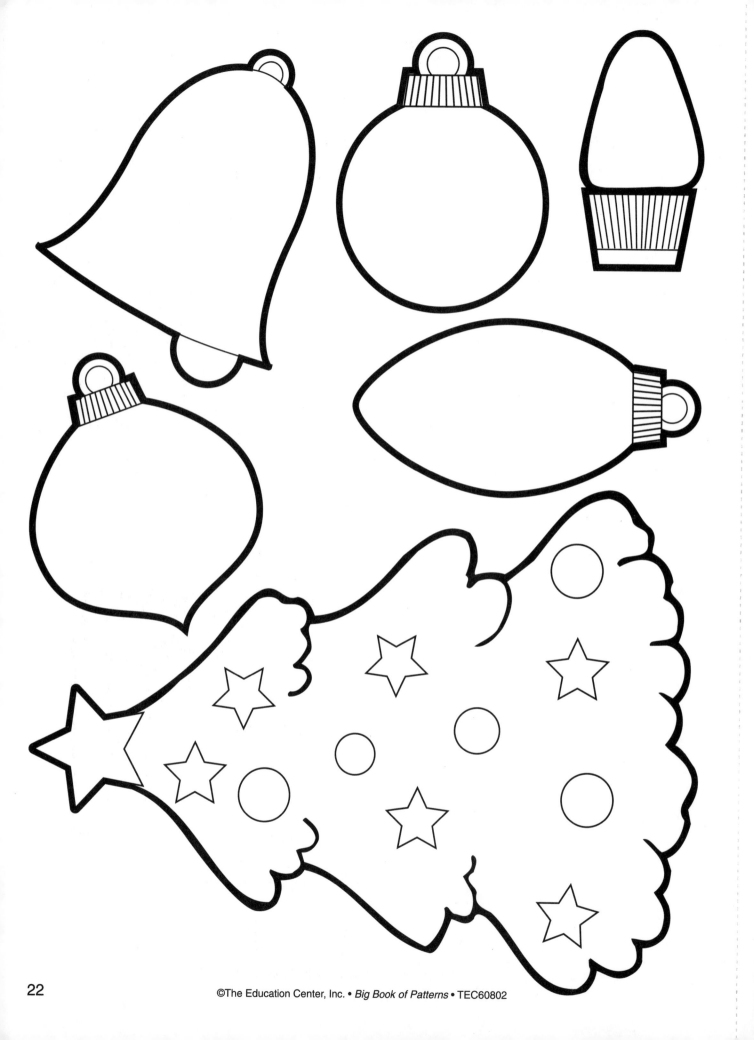

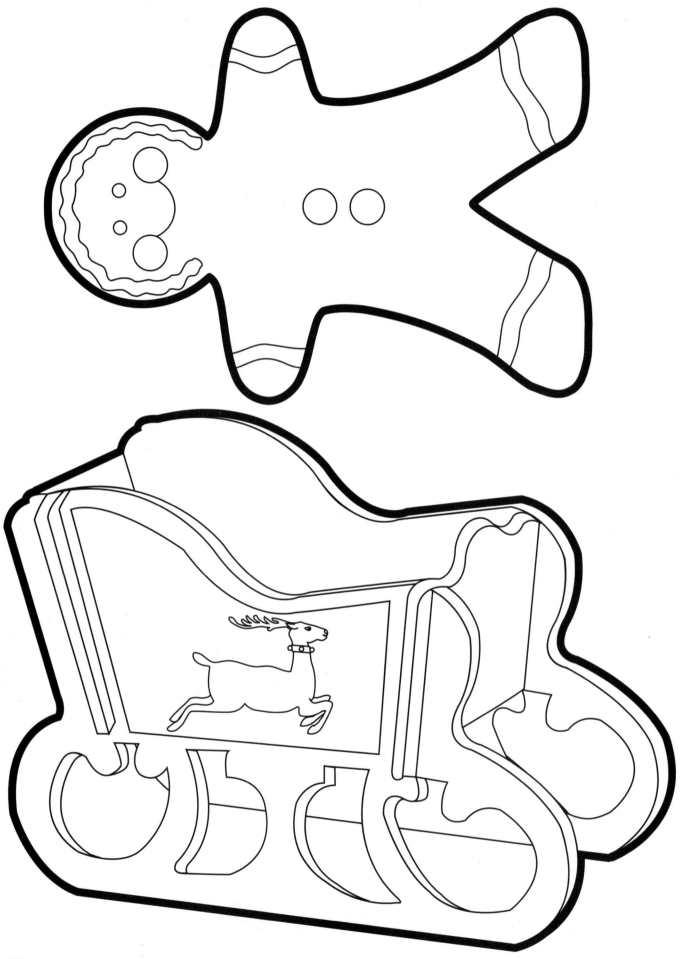

Circus

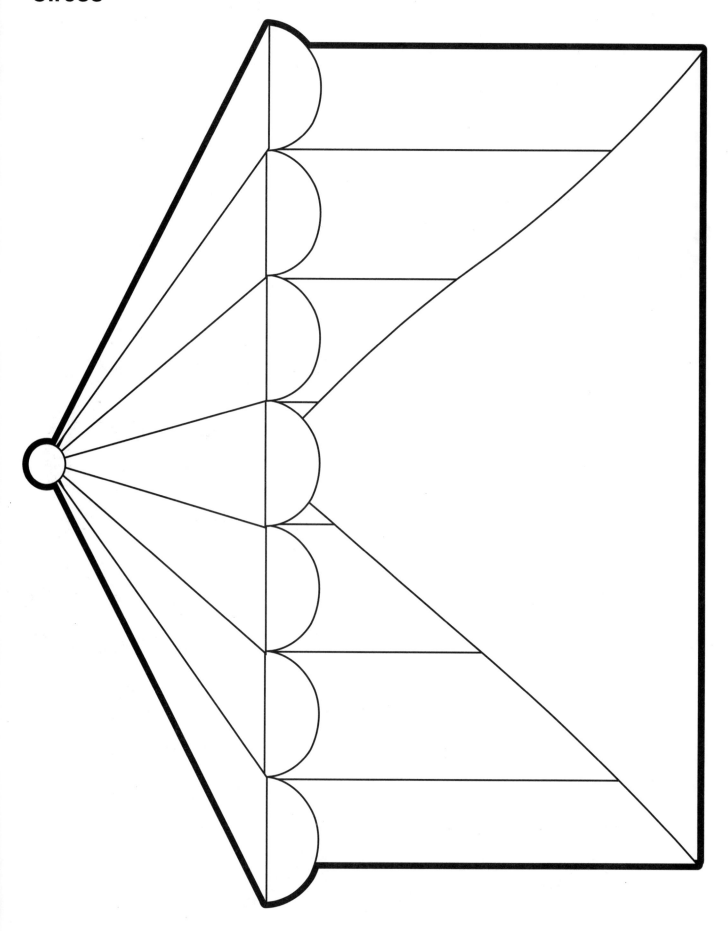

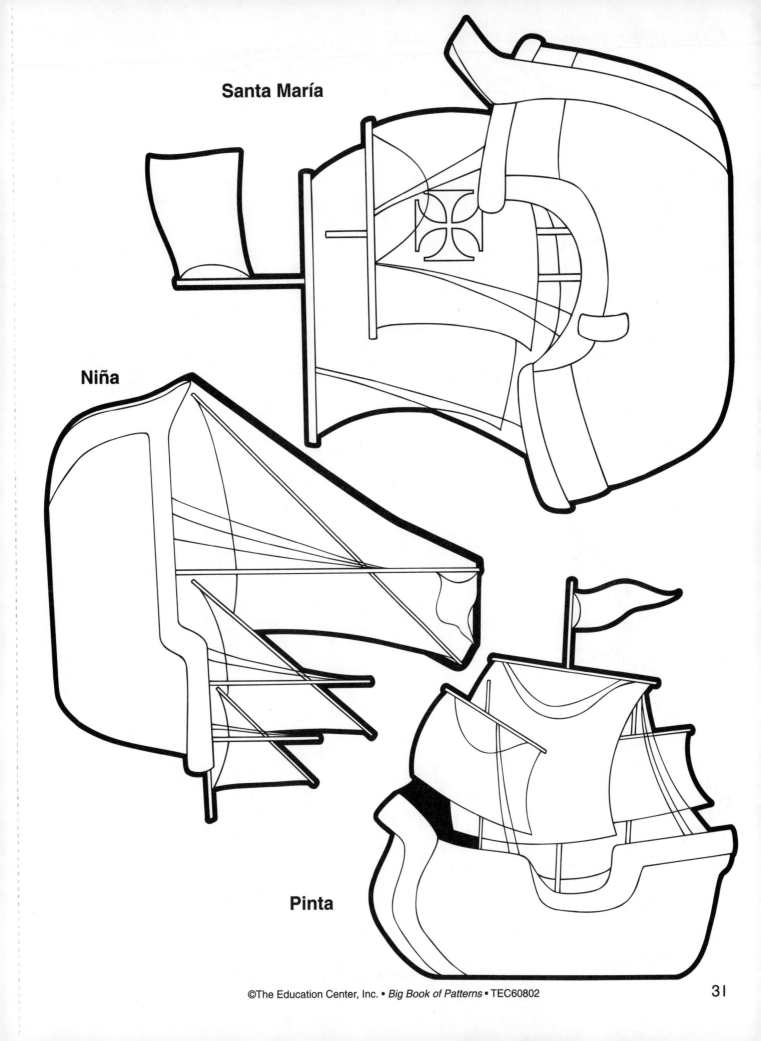

Santa María

Niña

Pinta

Community Helpers and Careers

firefighter

doctor

mail carrier

sanitation worker

librarian

police officer

Check Out

POLICE OFFICER

Dinosaurs

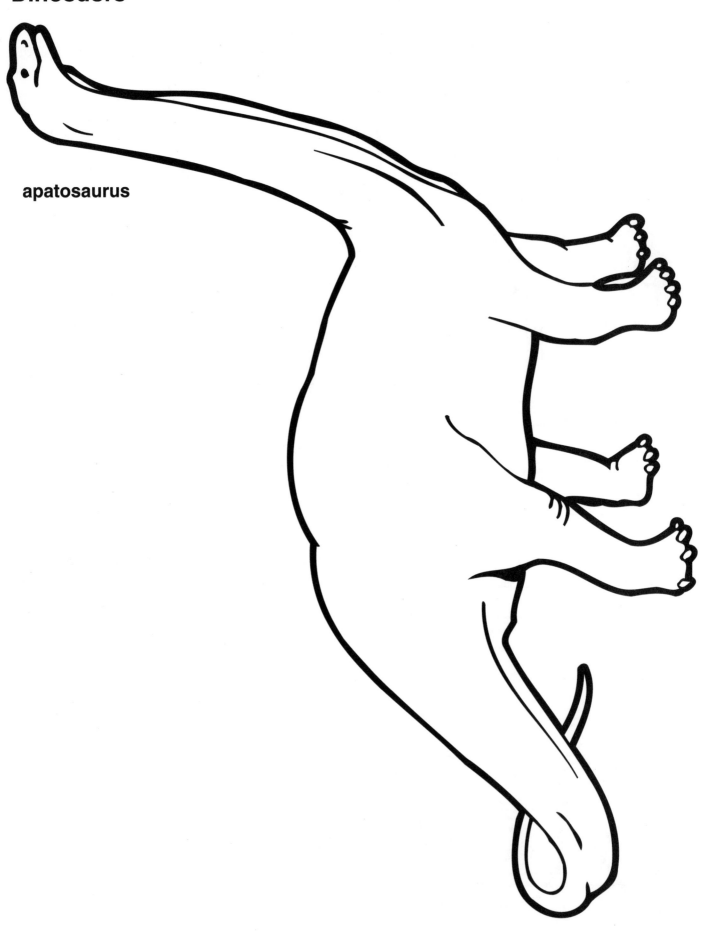

apatosaurus

stegosaurus

triceratops

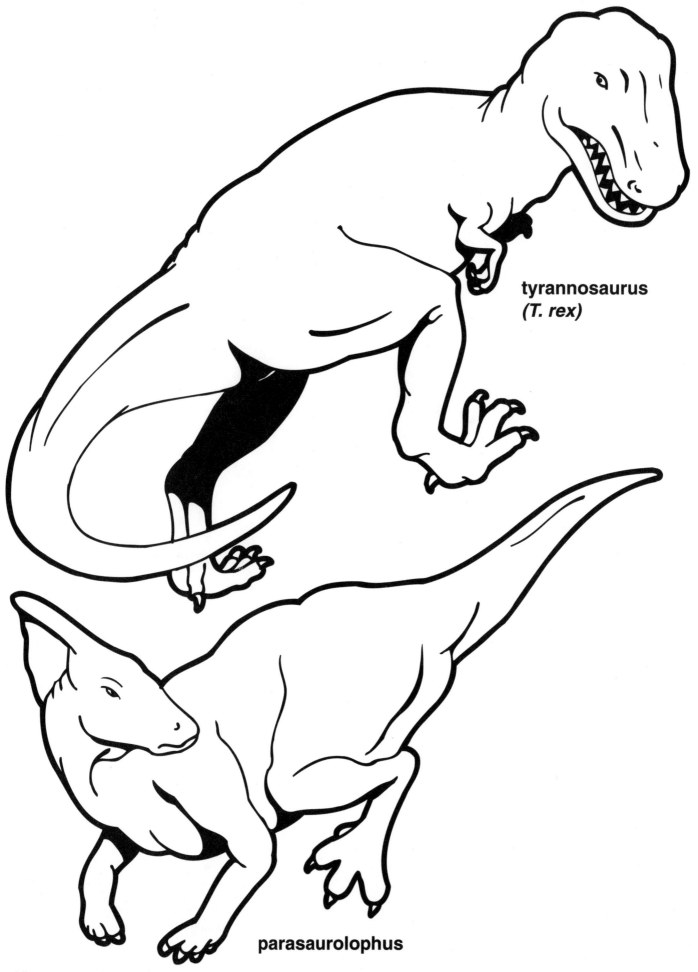

**tyrannosaurus
(T. rex)**

parasaurolophus

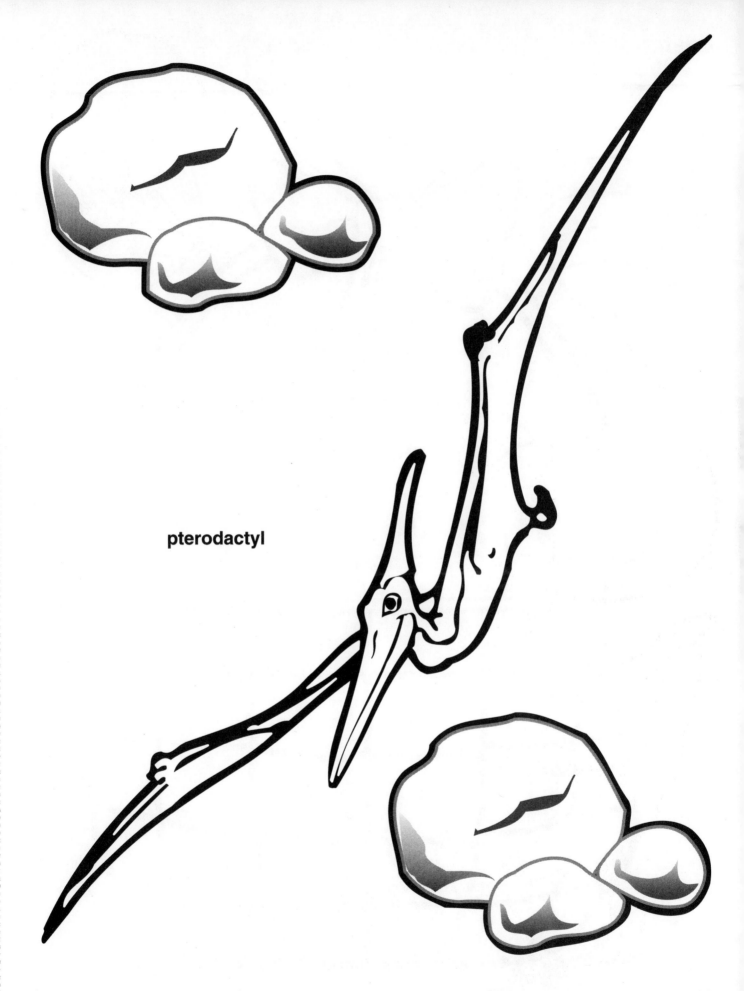

pterodactyl

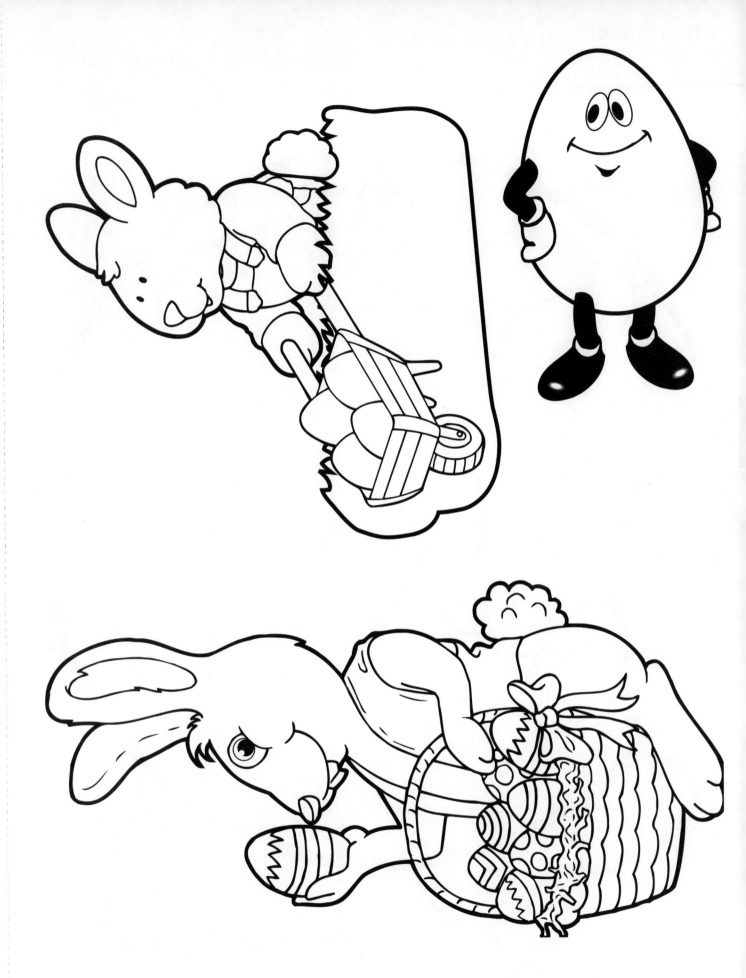

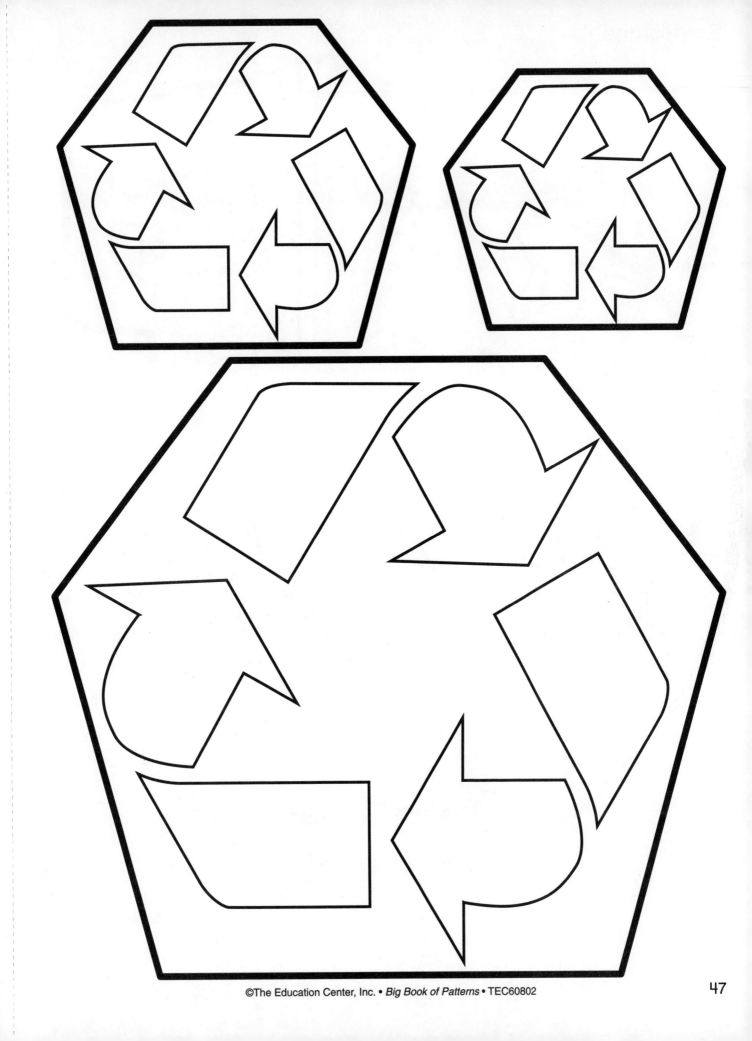

48 ©The Education Center, Inc. • *Big Book of Patterns* • TEC60802

50 ©The Education Center, Inc. • *Big Book of Patterns* • TEC60802

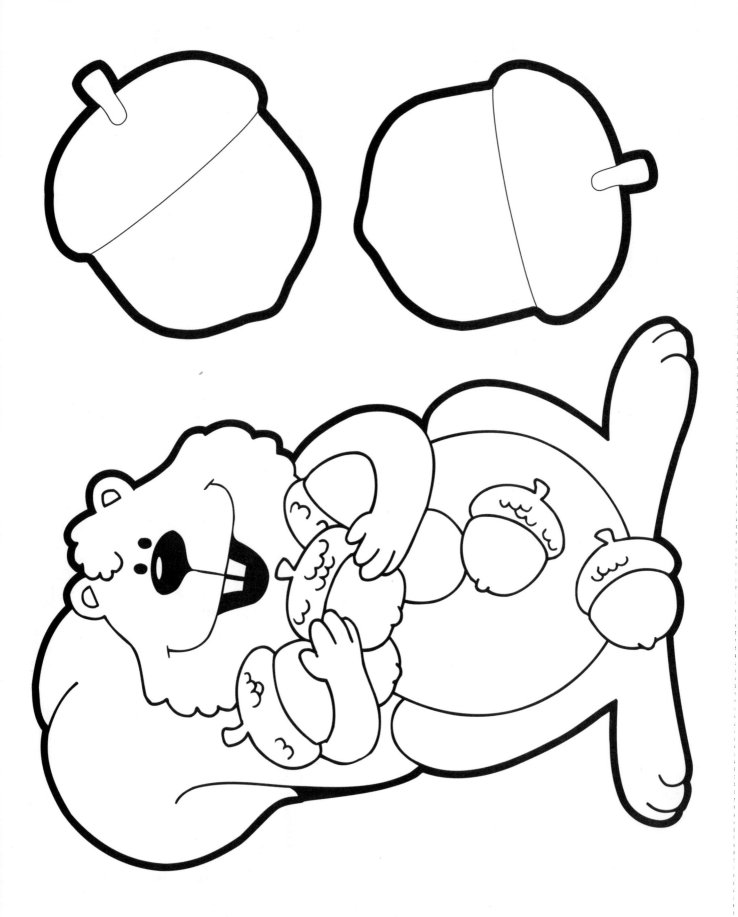

Farm

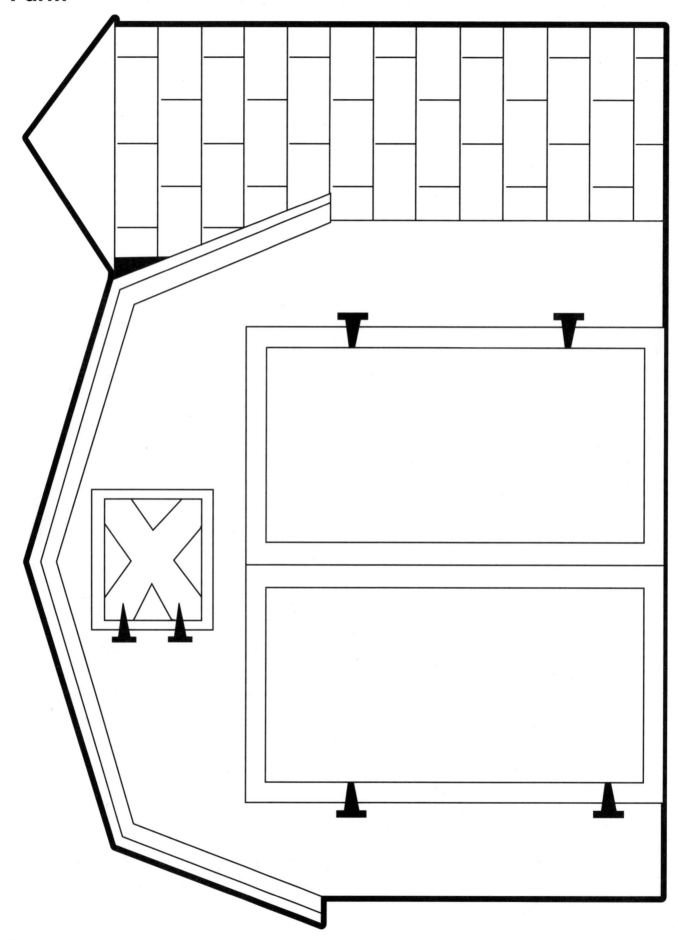

Geometry

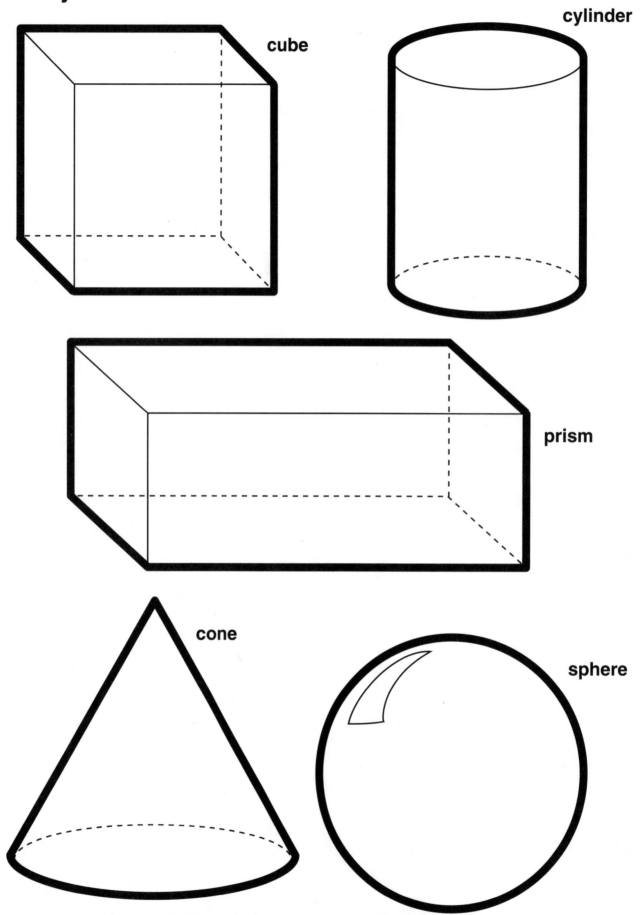

cube

cylinder

prism

cone

sphere

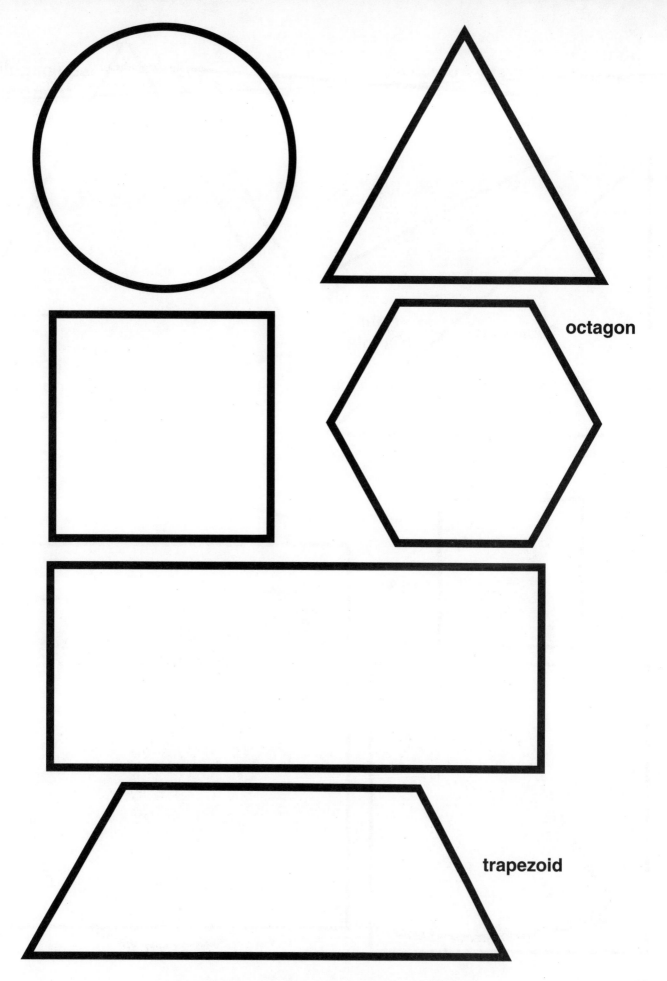

octagon

trapezoid

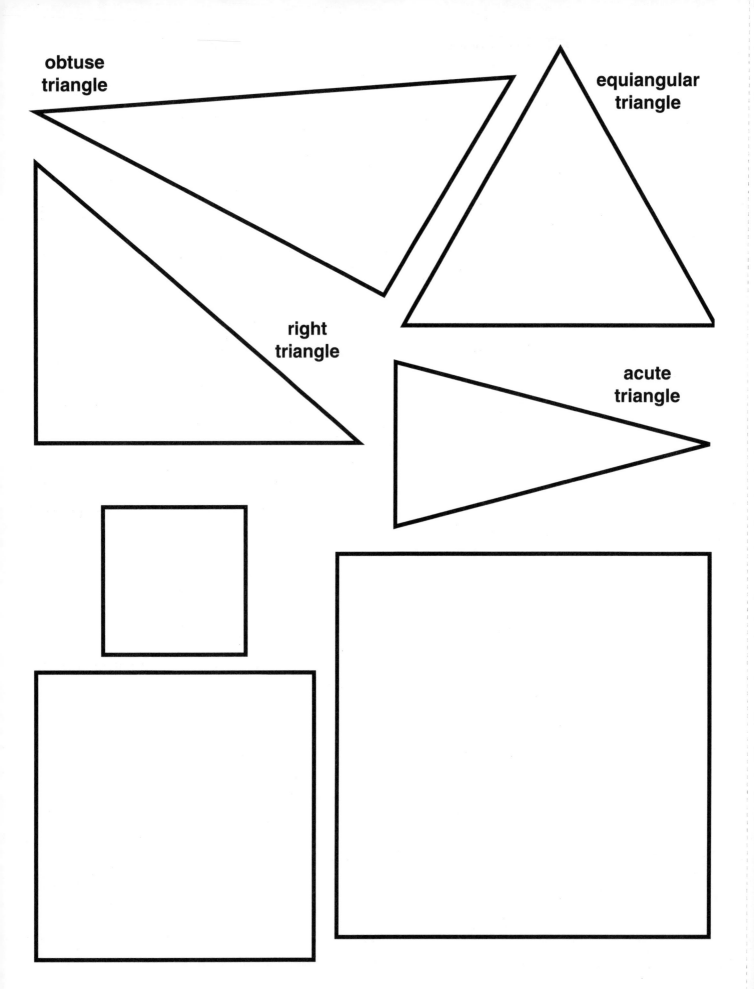

obtuse
triangle

equiangular
triangle

right
triangle

acute
triangle

octagon

trapezoid

parallelogram

tangram

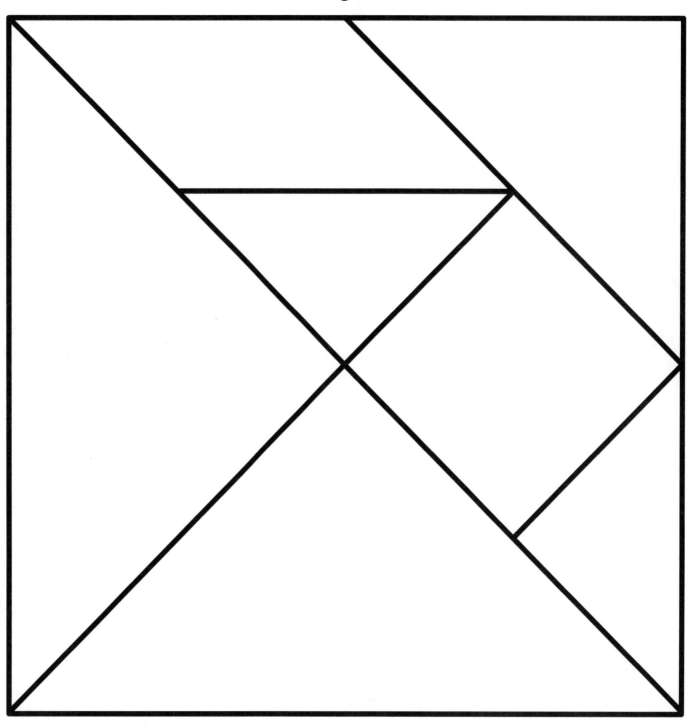

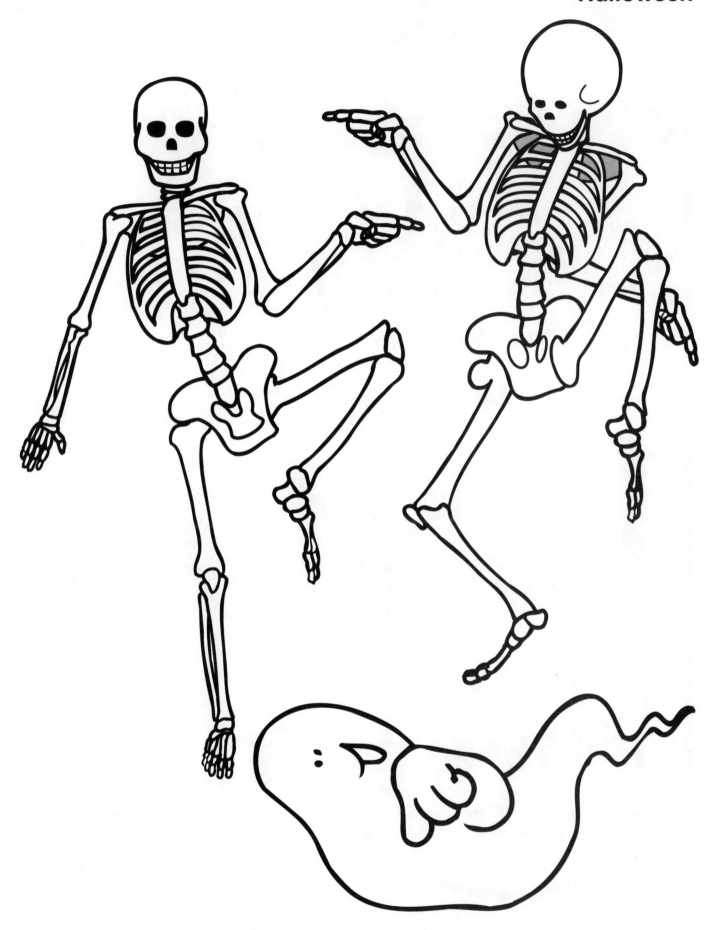

TRICK OR TREAT!

74 ©The Education Center, Inc. • *Big Book of Patterns* • TEC60802

"Boo-tiful" Work!

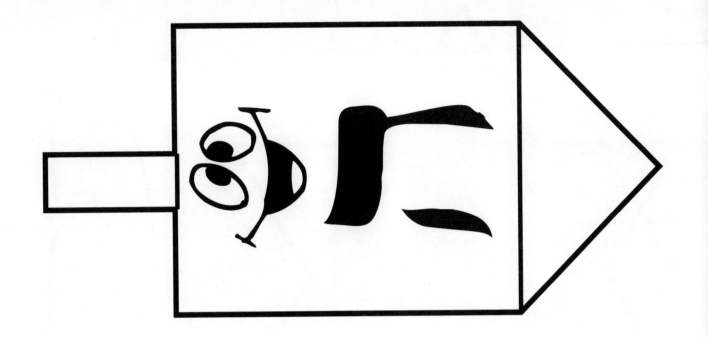

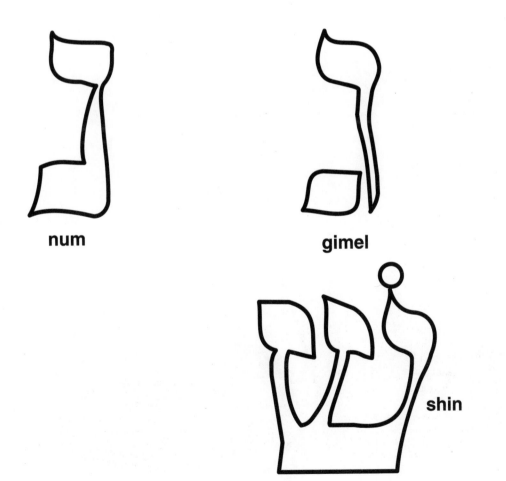

num

gimel

hay

shin

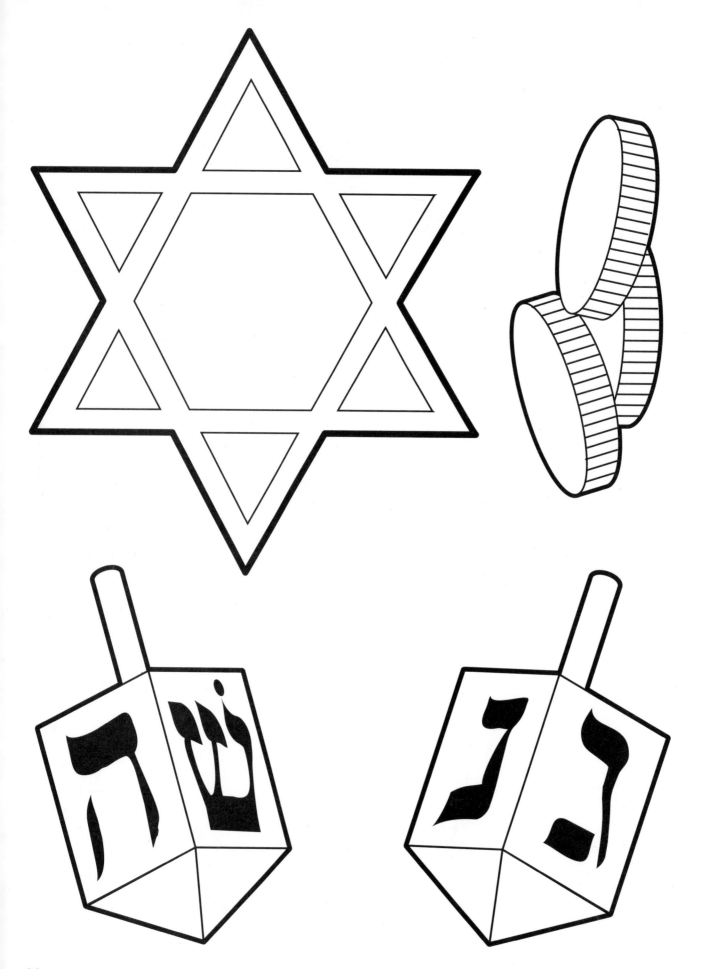

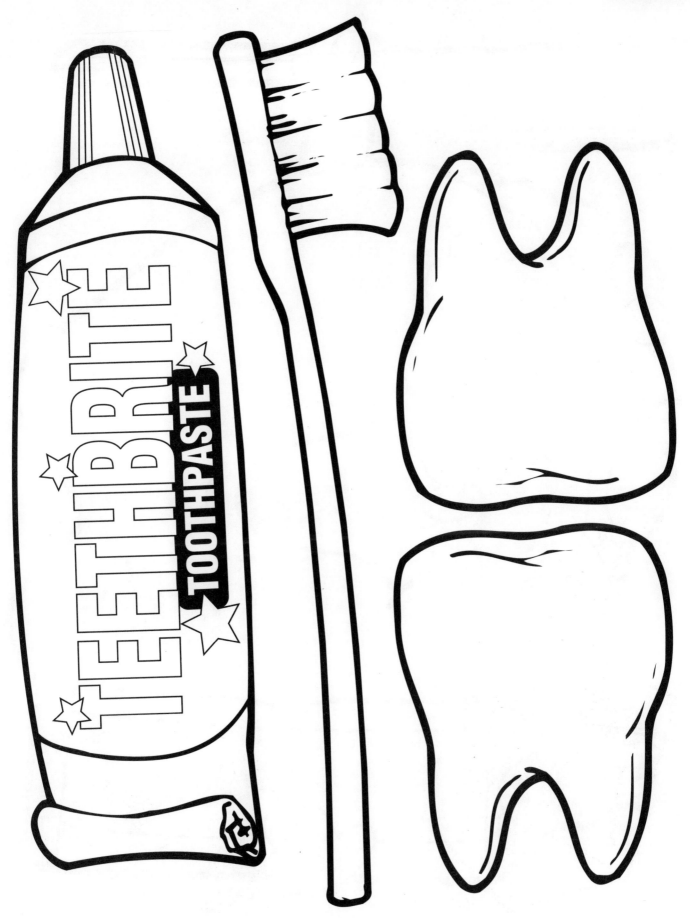

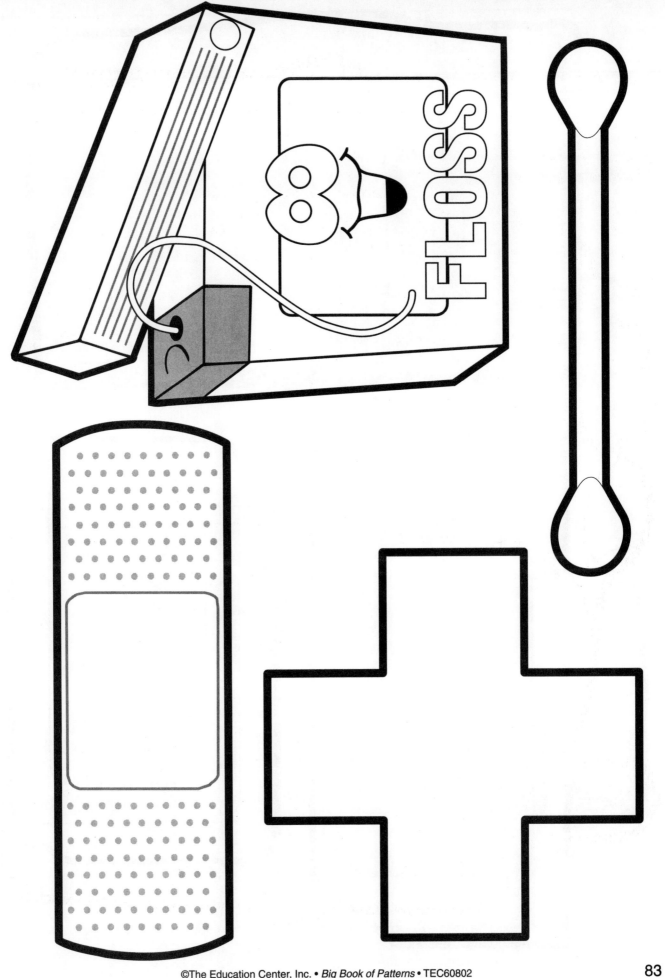

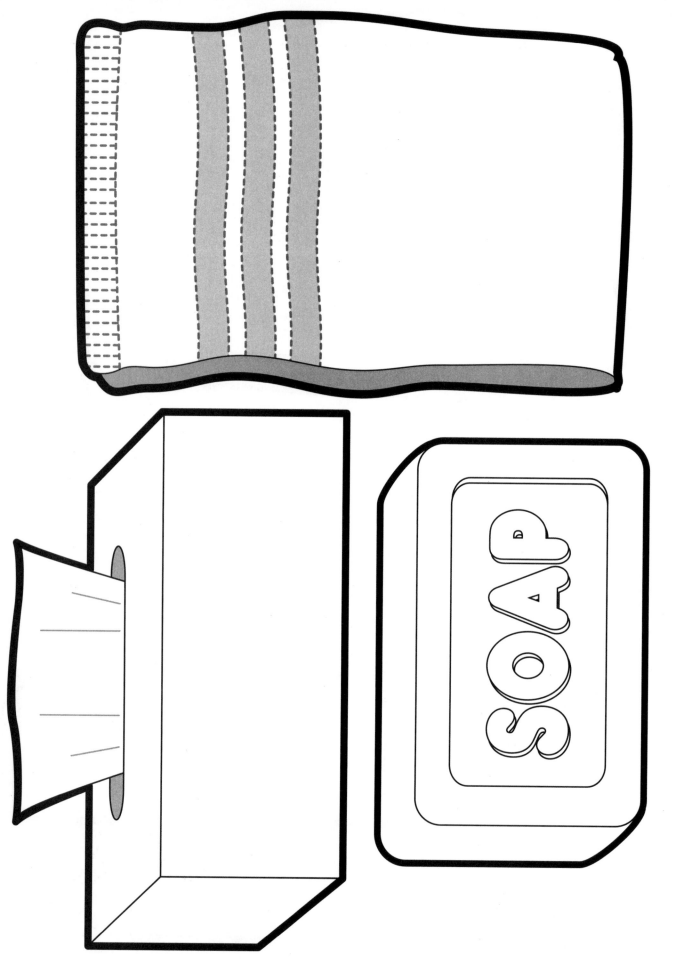

84

Insects

butterfly

caterpillar

ant

ladybug

fly

beetle

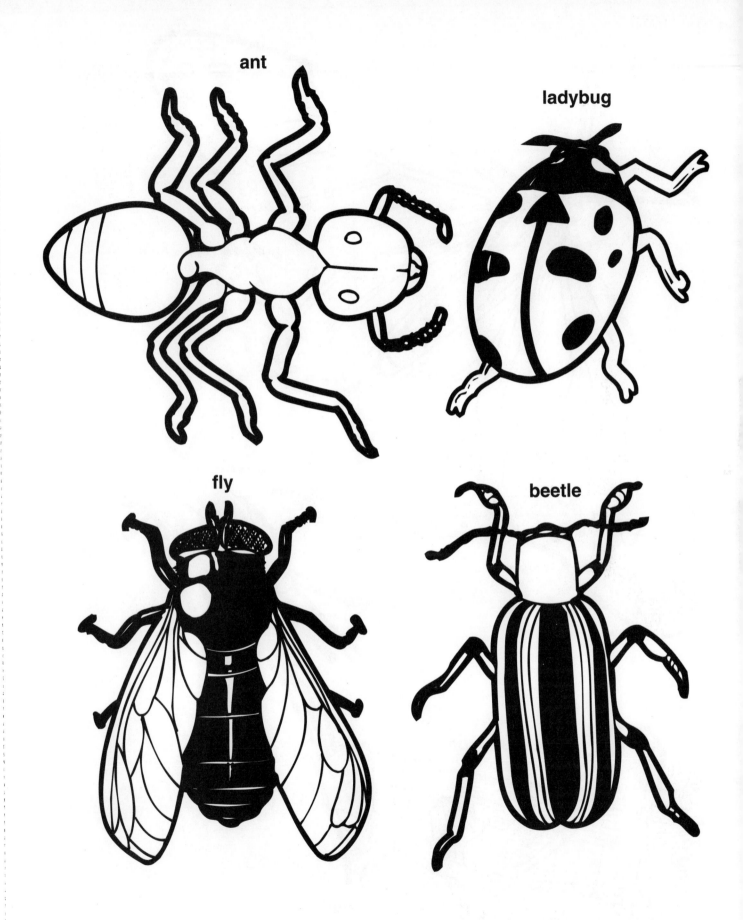

moth

cricket

grasshopper

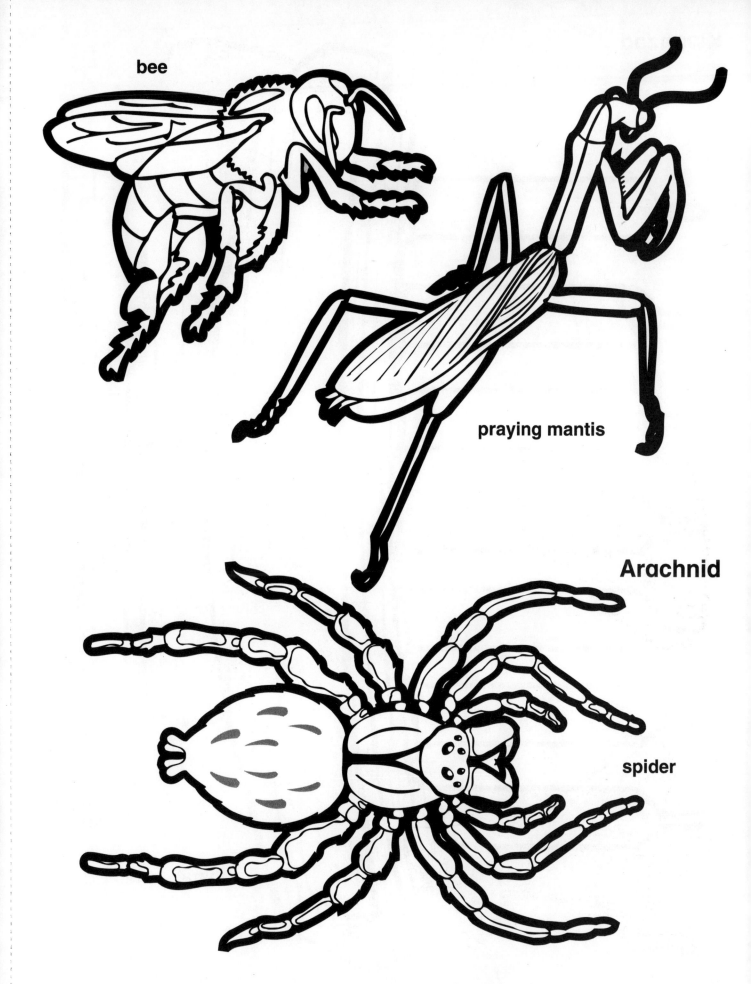

bee

praying mantis

Arachnid

spider

Kwanzaa

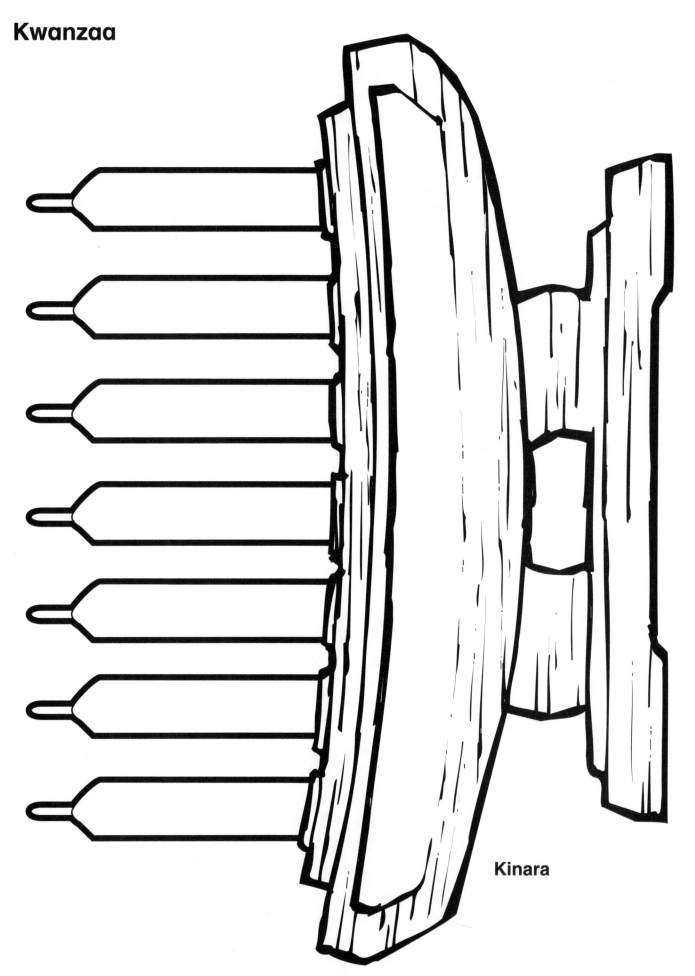

Kinara

Unity Cup

Mkeka

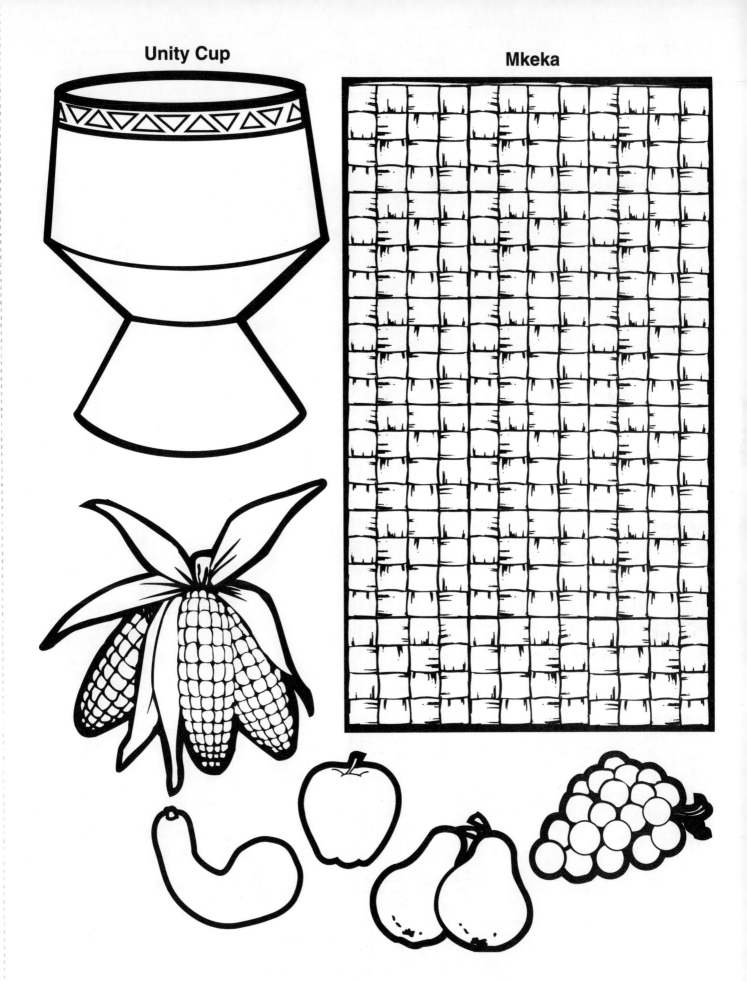

May Your **KWANZAA** Be Happy!

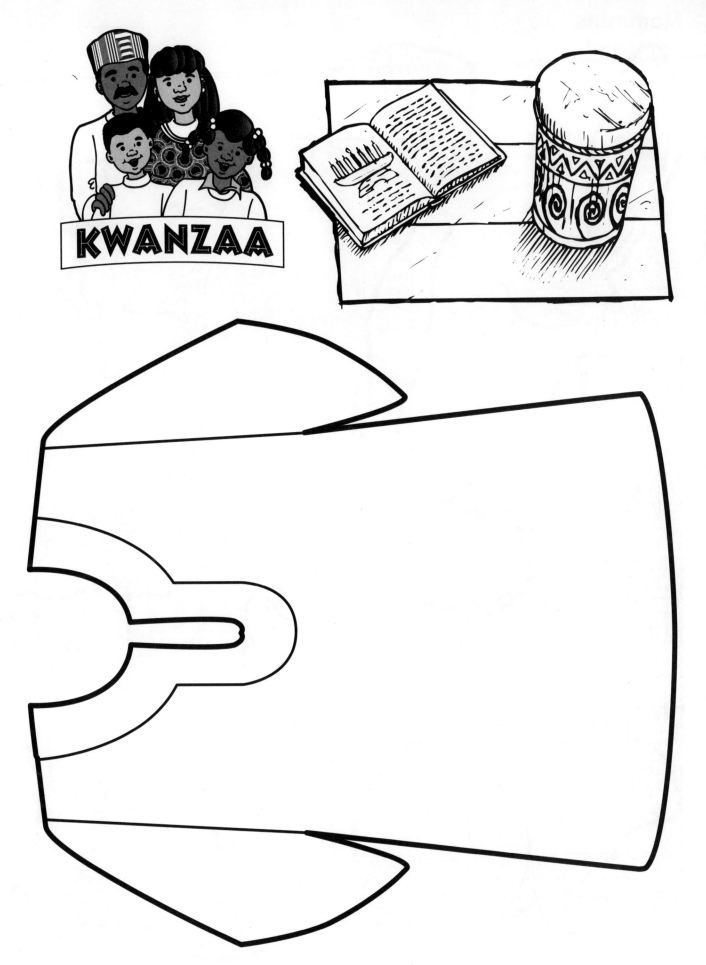

KWANZAA

Mammals

gorilla

beaver

mouse

cat

rabbit

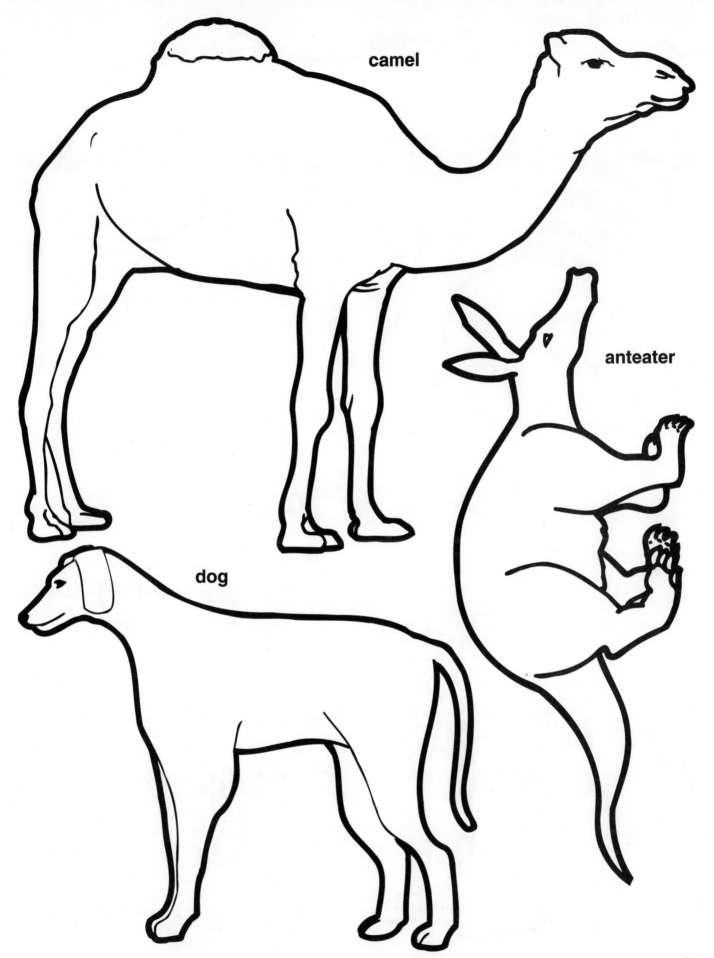

camel

anteater

dog

hippopotamus

raccoon

cheetah

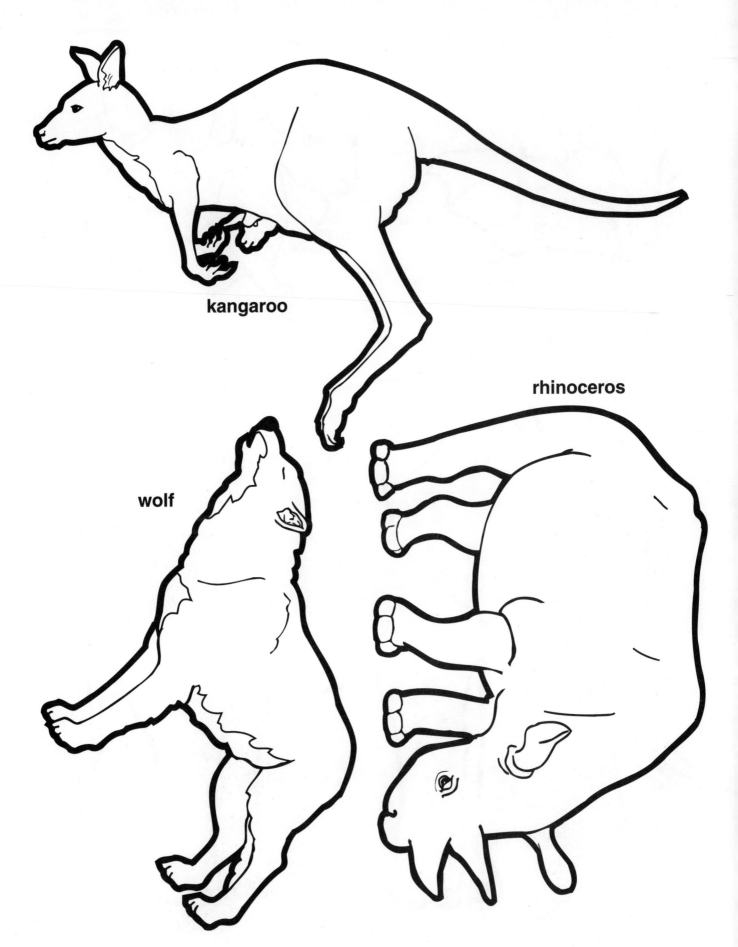

kangaroo

rhinoceros

wolf

bat

squirrel

elephant

horse

giraffe

Martin Luther King Jr.

Math Patterns

1	2	3	4	5	6	7	8	9	10
11	12	13	14	15	16	17	18	19	20
21	22	23	24	25	26	27	28	29	30
31	32	33	34	35	36	37	38	39	40
41	42	43	44	45	46	47	48	49	50
51	52	53	54	55	56	57	58	59	60
61	62	63	64	65	66	67	68	69	70
71	72	73	74	75	76	77	78	79	80
81	82	83	84	85	86	87	88	89	90
91	92	93	94	95	96	97	98	99	100

billions			millions			thousands			ones		
H	T	O	H	T	O	H	T	O	H	T	O

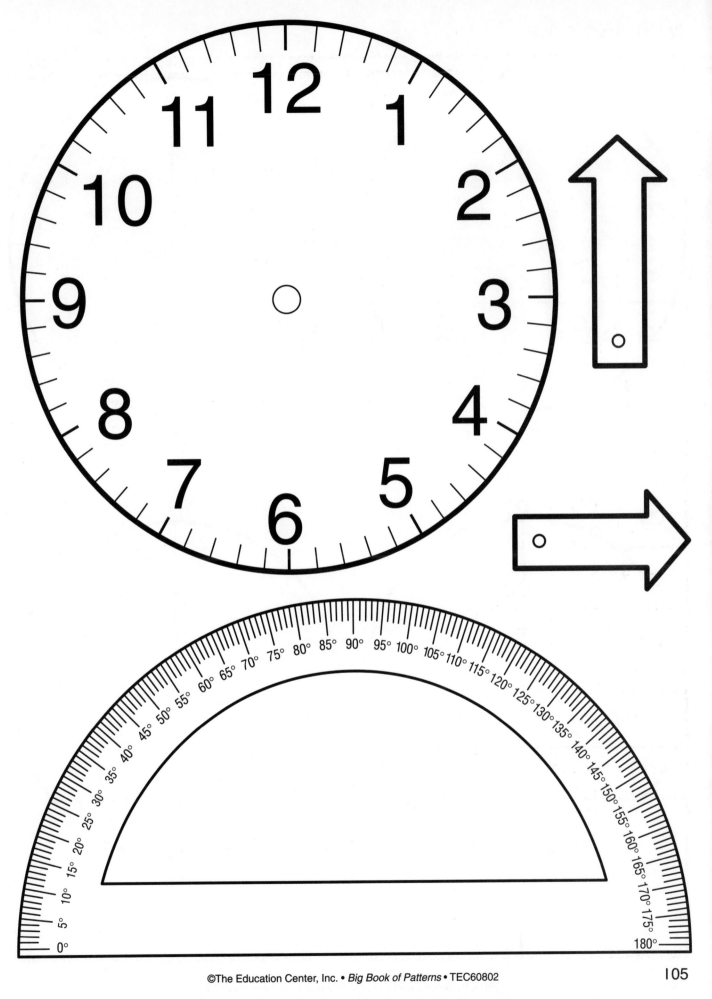

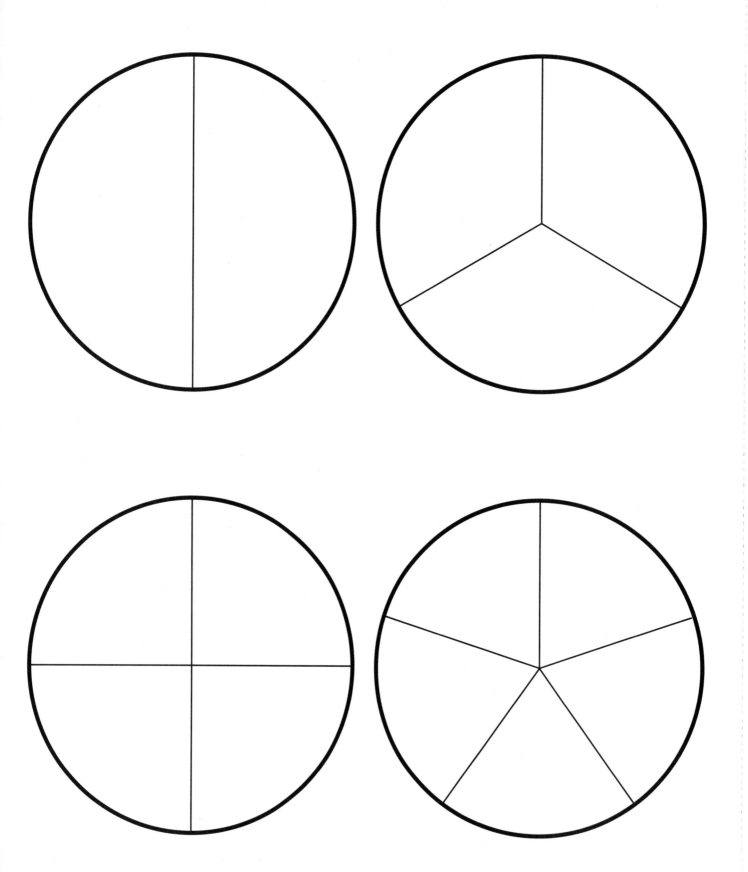

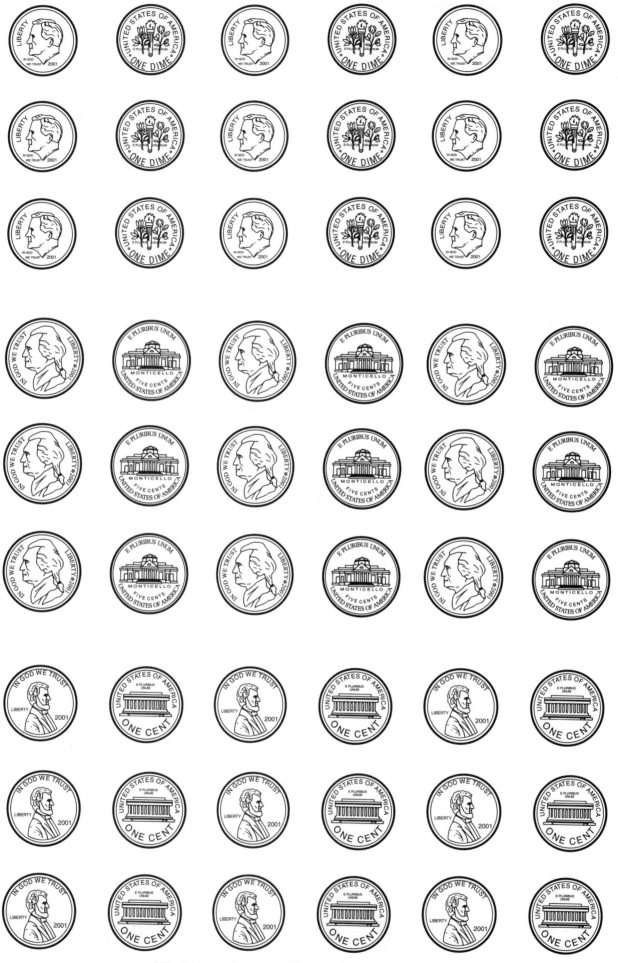

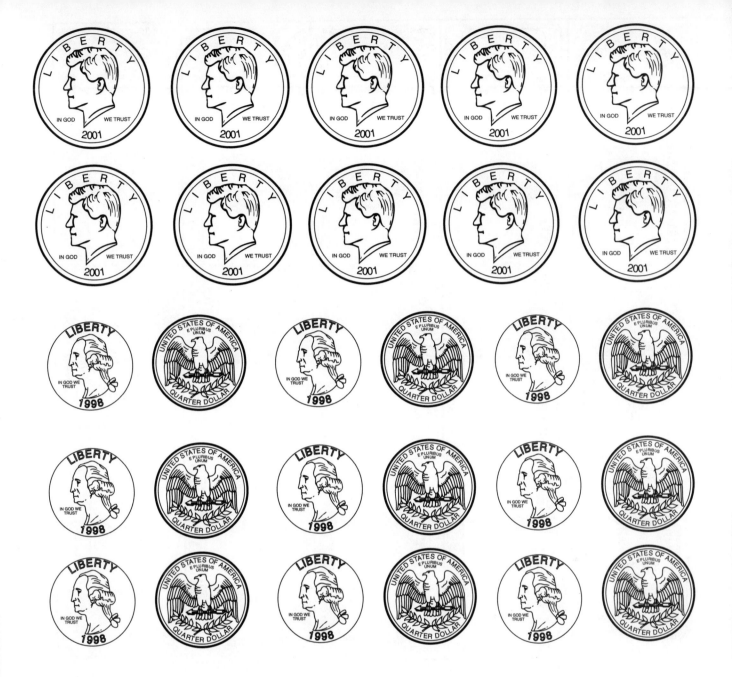

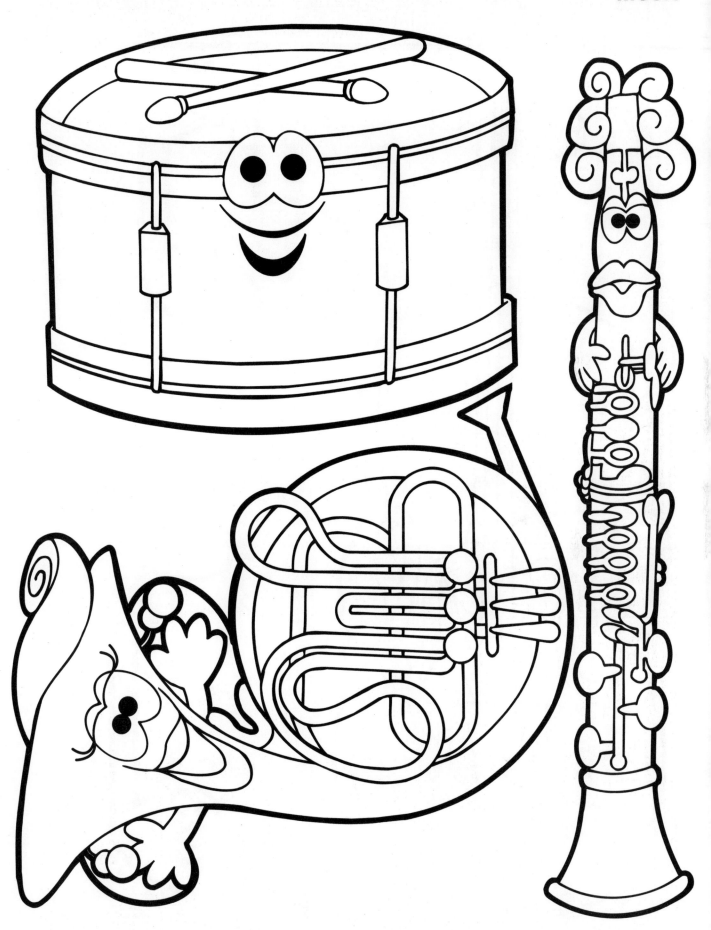

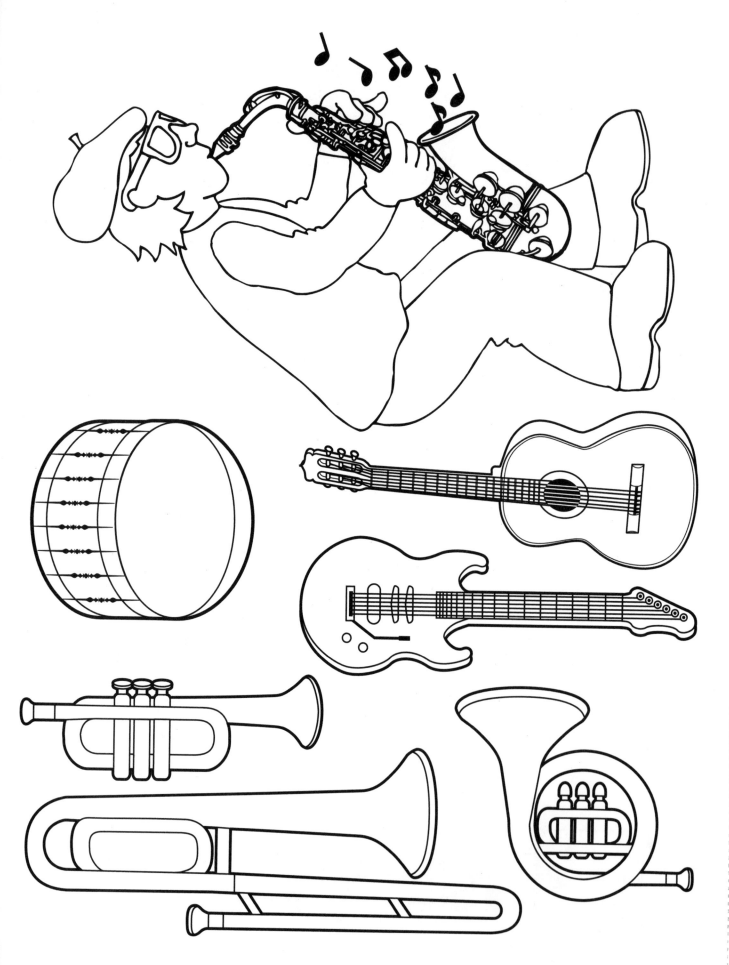

116

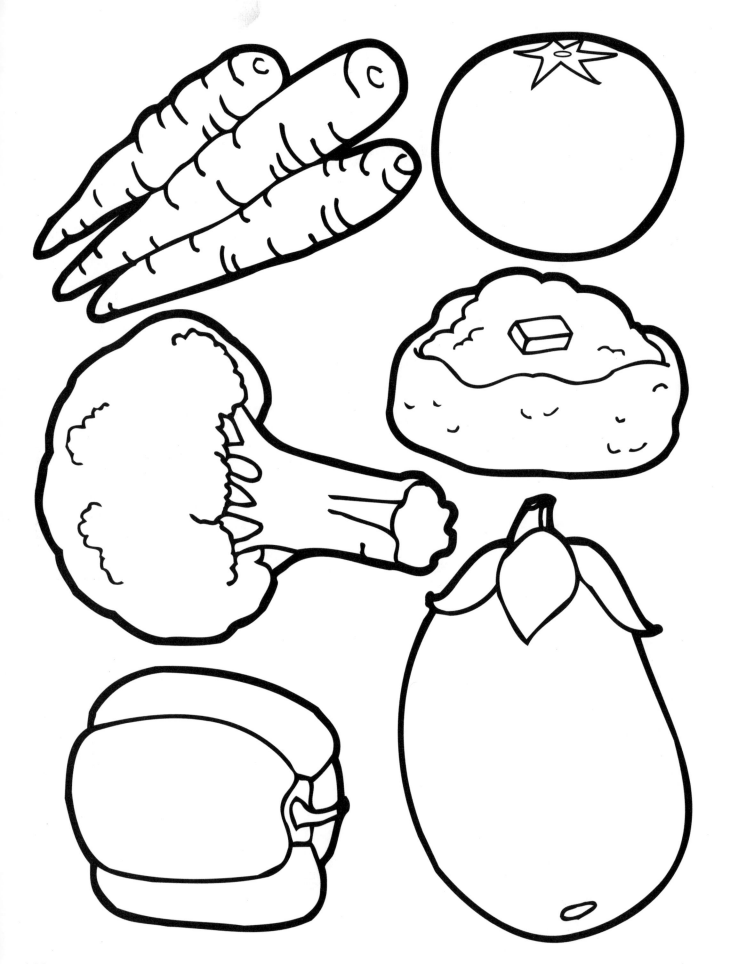

PASTA

124

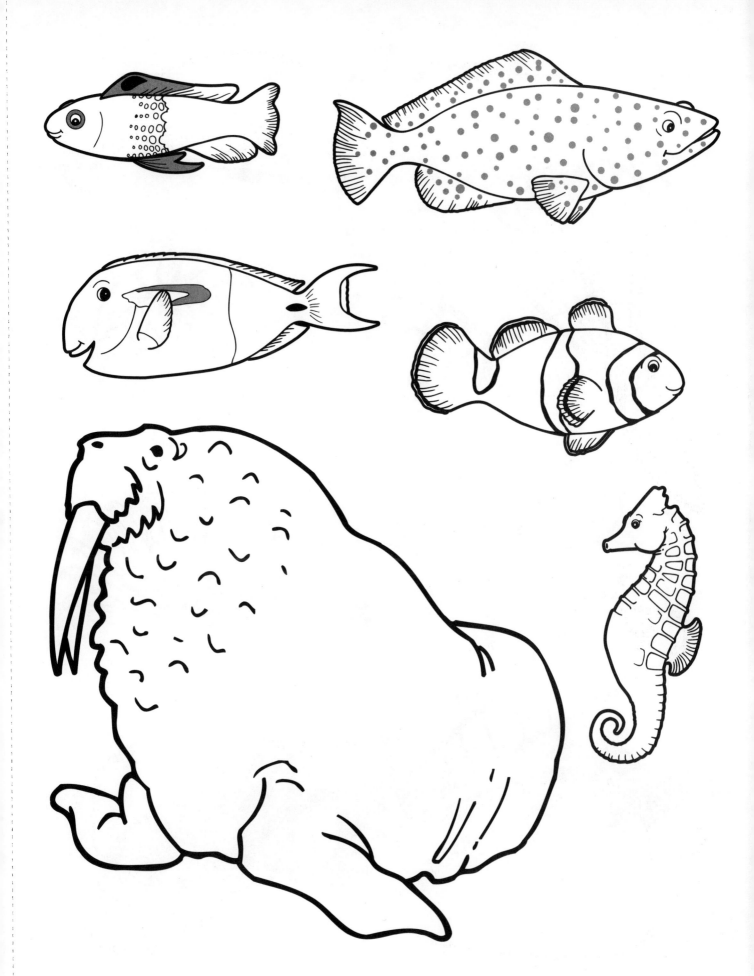

130 ©The Education Center, Inc. • *Big Book of Patterns* • TEC60802

132

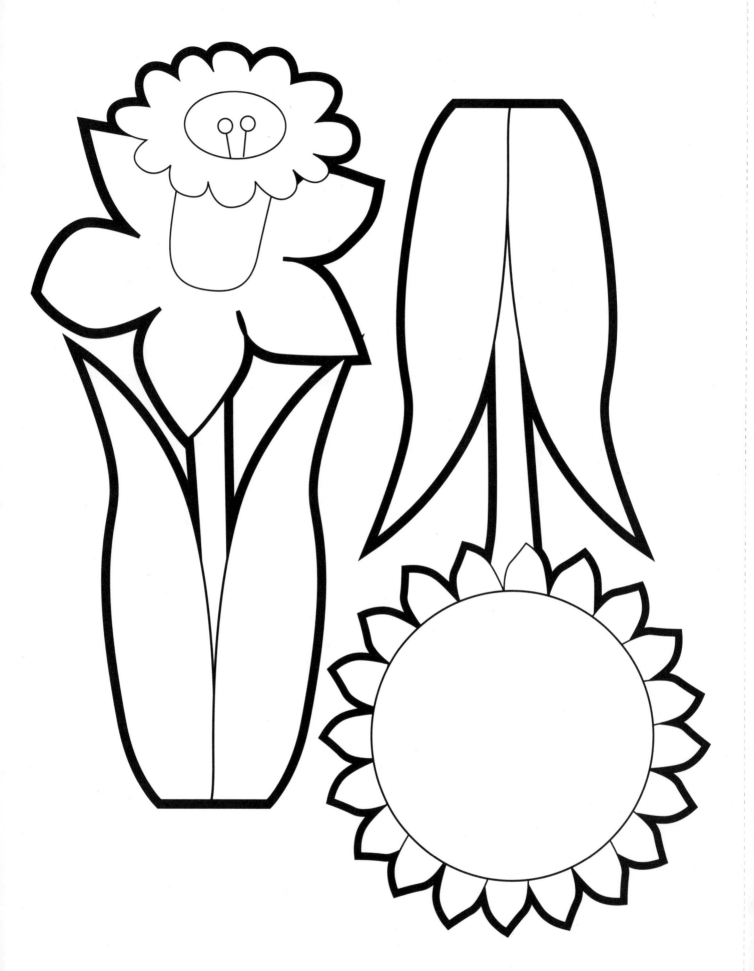

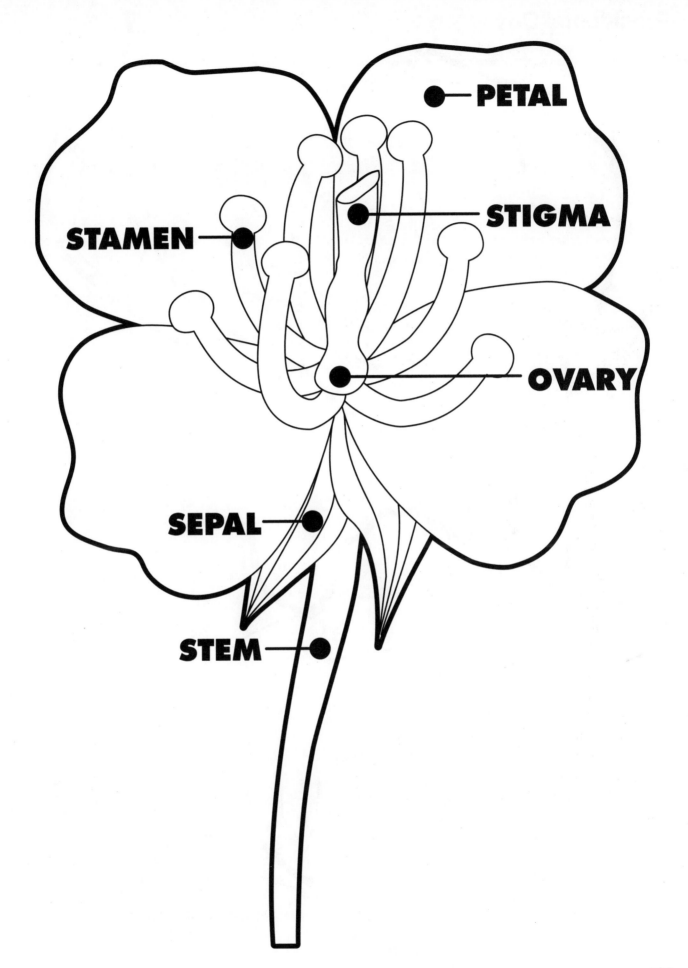

PETAL

STIGMA

STAMEN

OVARY

SEPAL

STEM

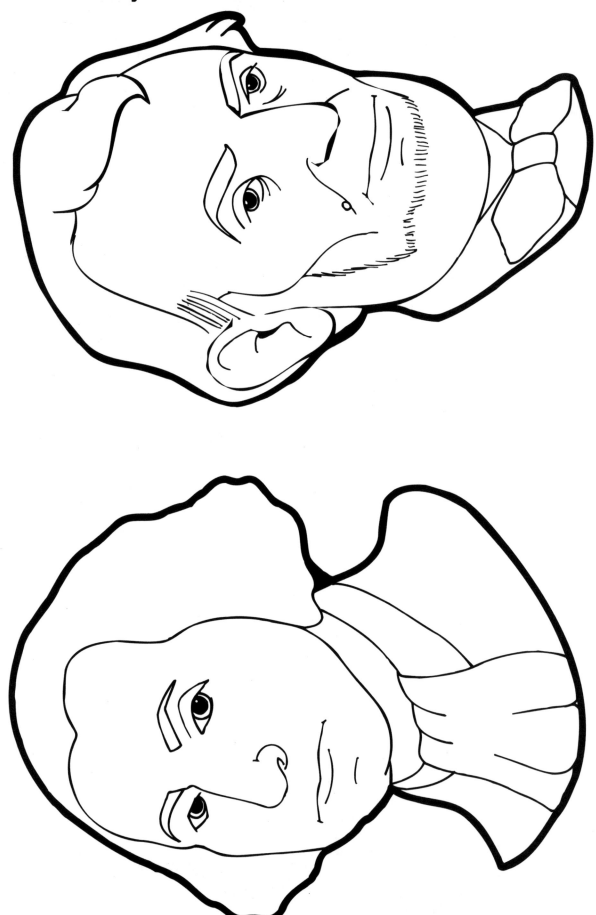

BIOGRAPHY

SCIENCE FICTION

MYSTERY

REALISTIC FICTION

140

Look Into Books!

Lamp of Knowledge

SOAR INTO READING!

143

144

Welcome Back!

147

148

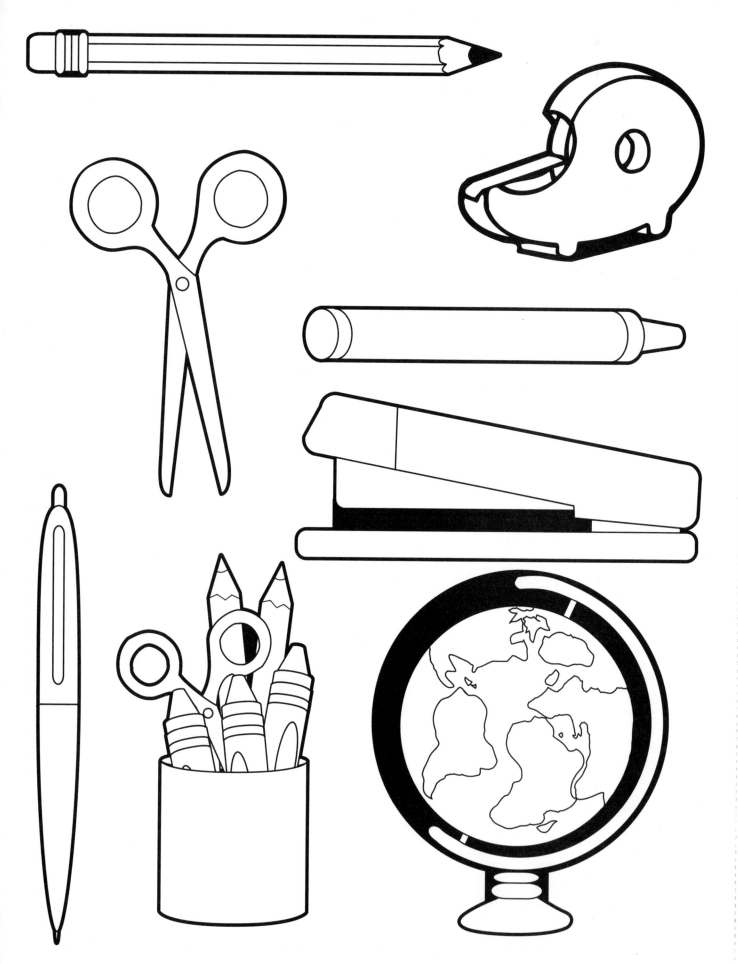

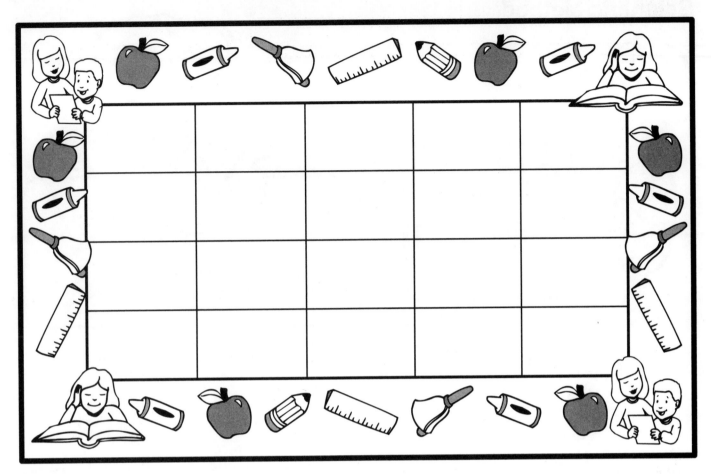

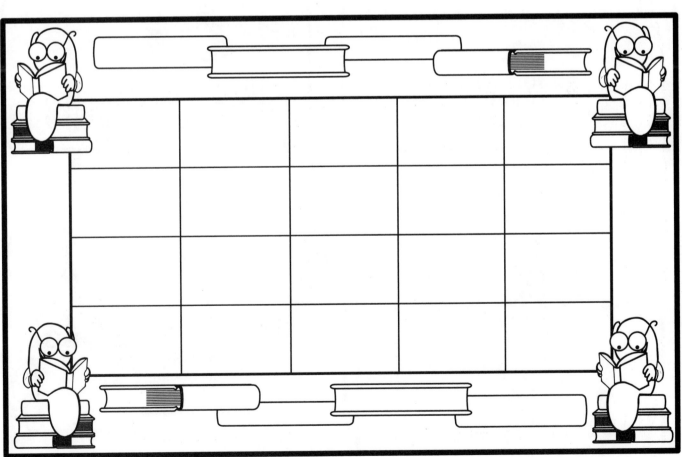

151

Scientific Method

Problem

Hypothesis

Materials

Procedure

Conclusion

Results

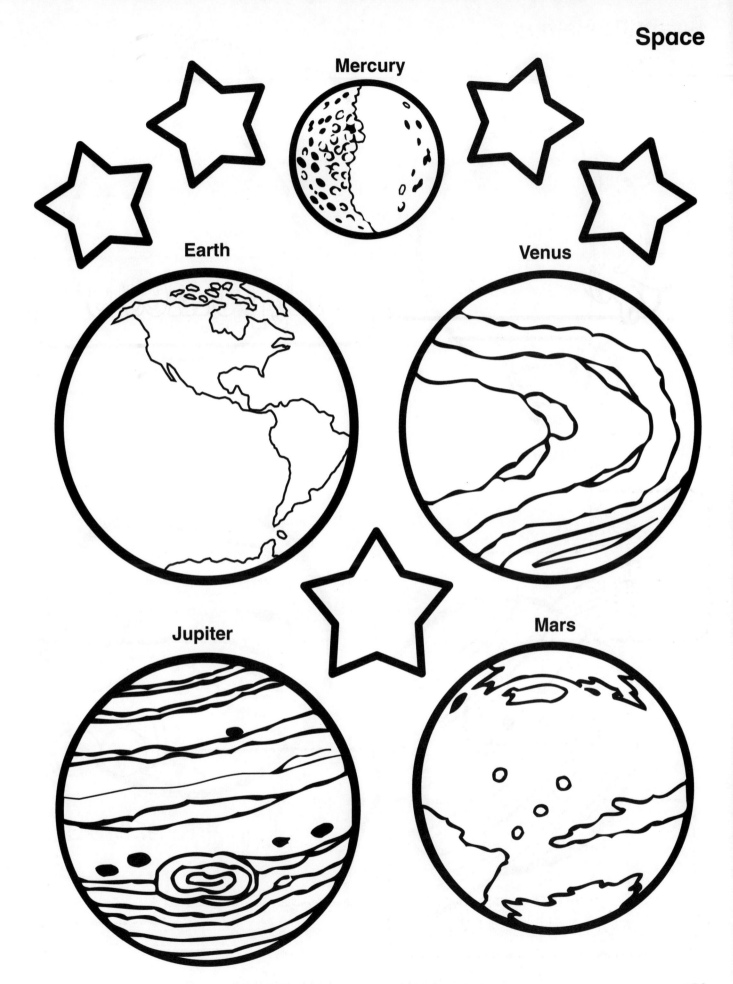

Mercury

Earth

Venus

Jupiter

Mars

153

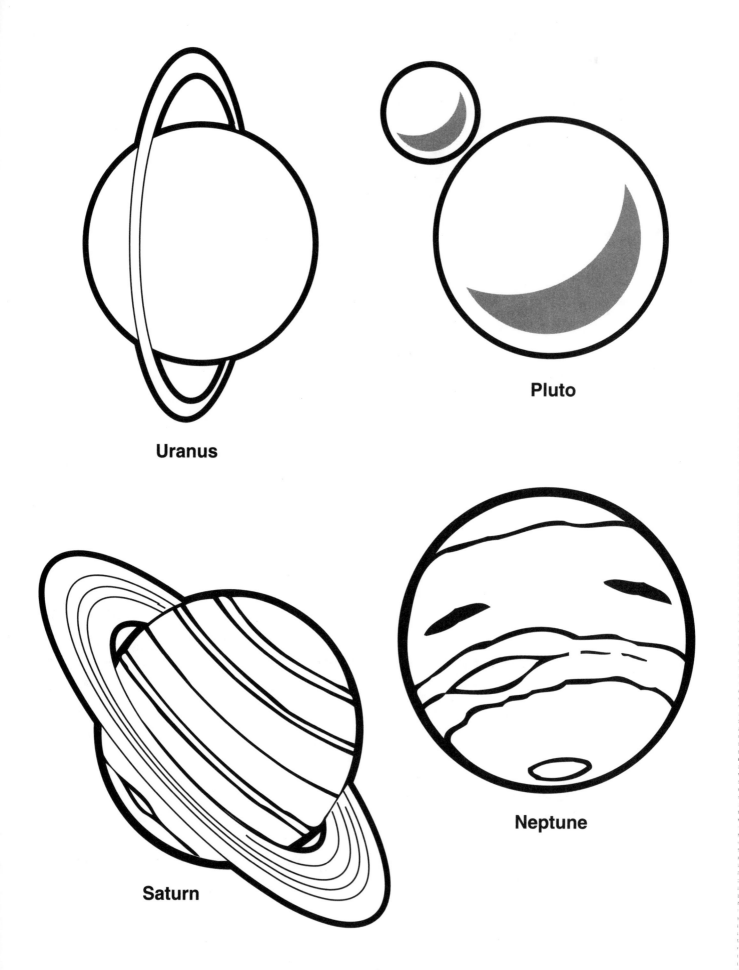

Uranus

Pluto

Saturn

Neptune

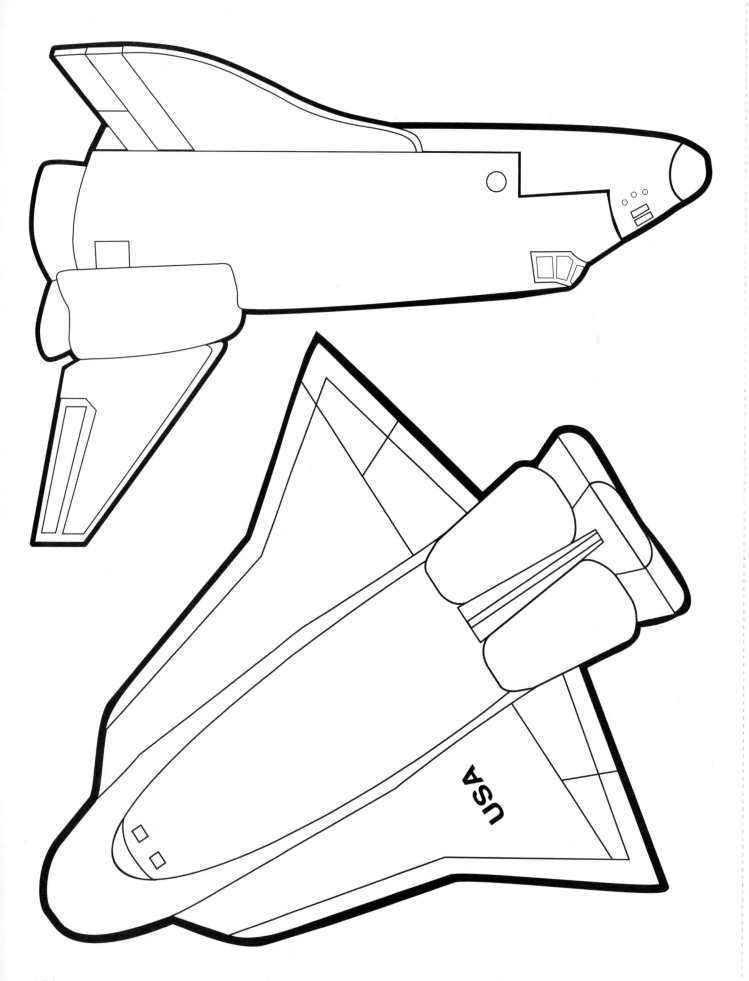

156

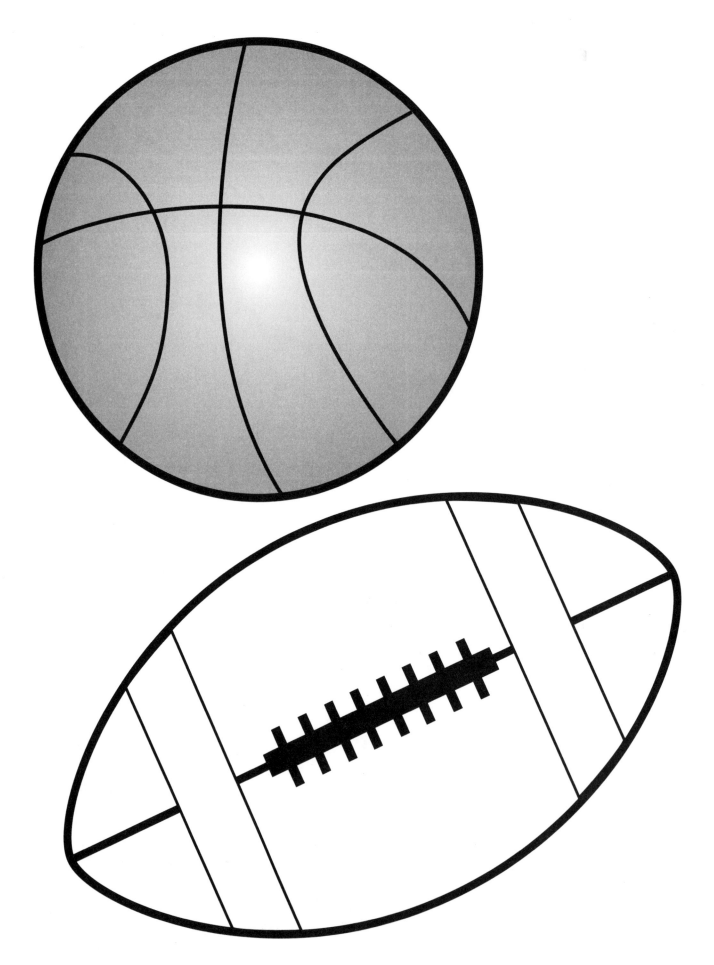

162 ©The Education Center, Inc. • *Big Book of Patterns* • TEC60802

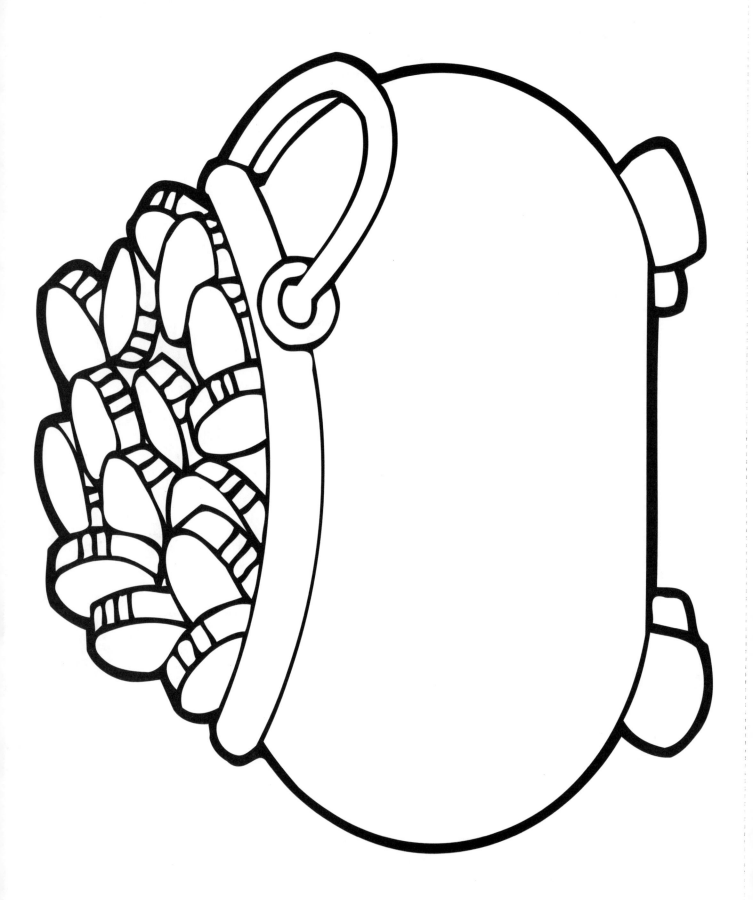

164

166

170

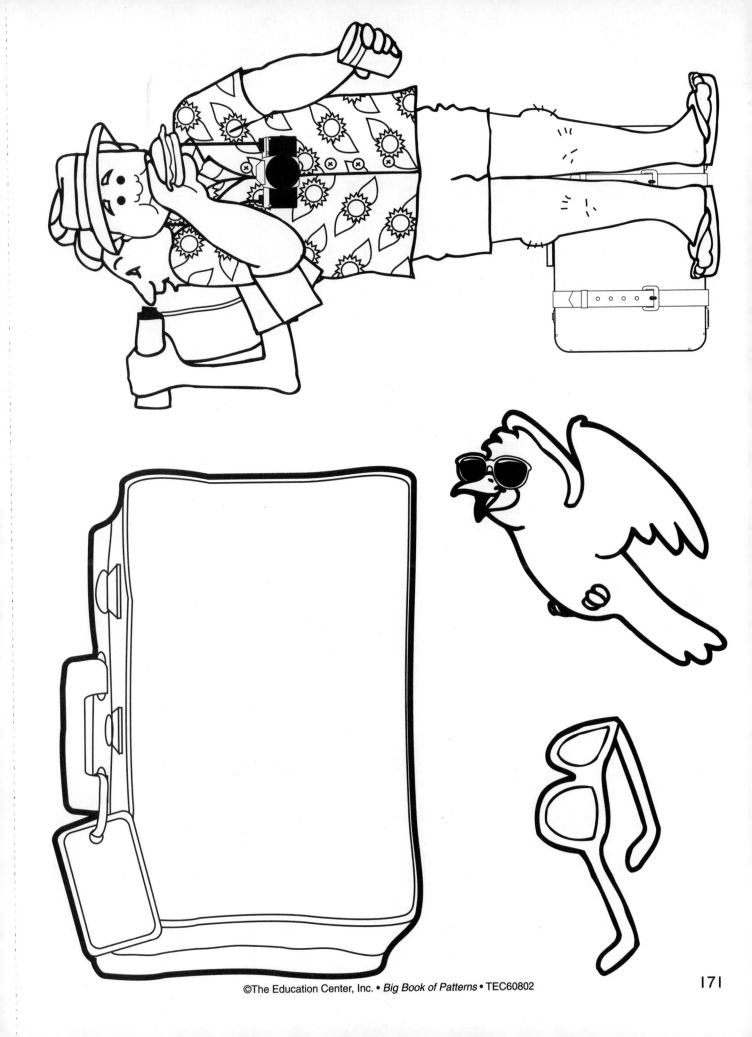

Technology

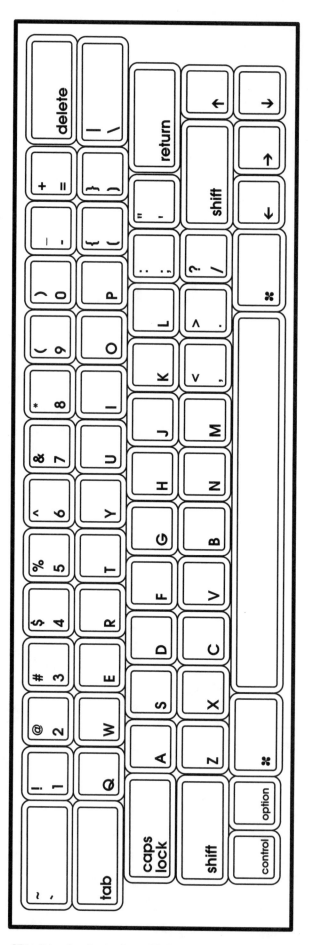

Thanksgiving

Mayflower

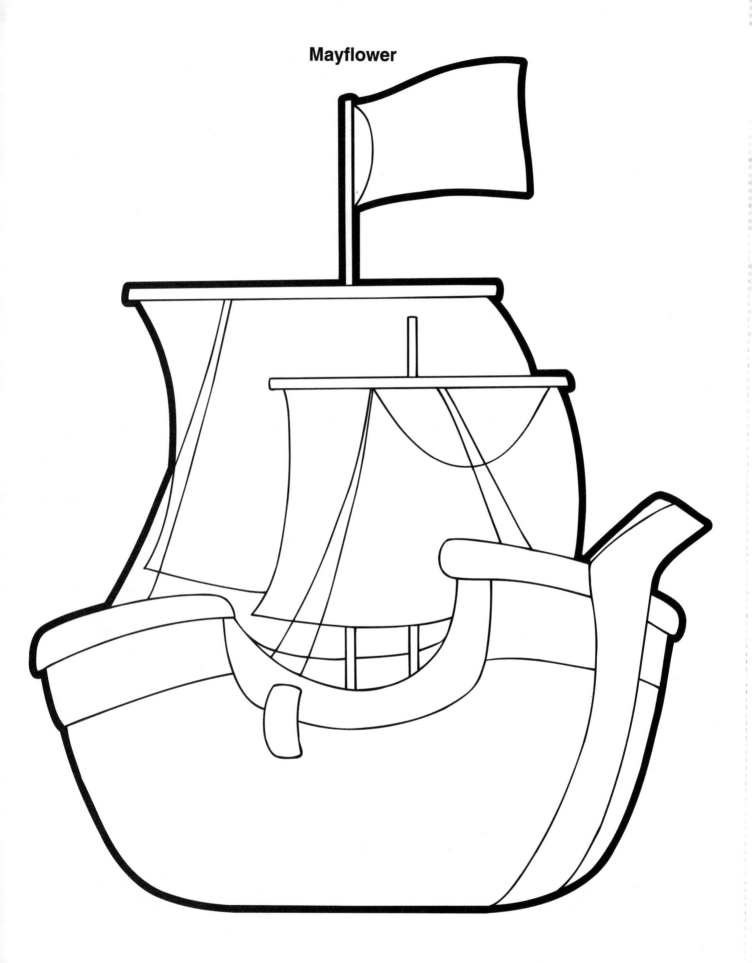

minute hand

hour hand

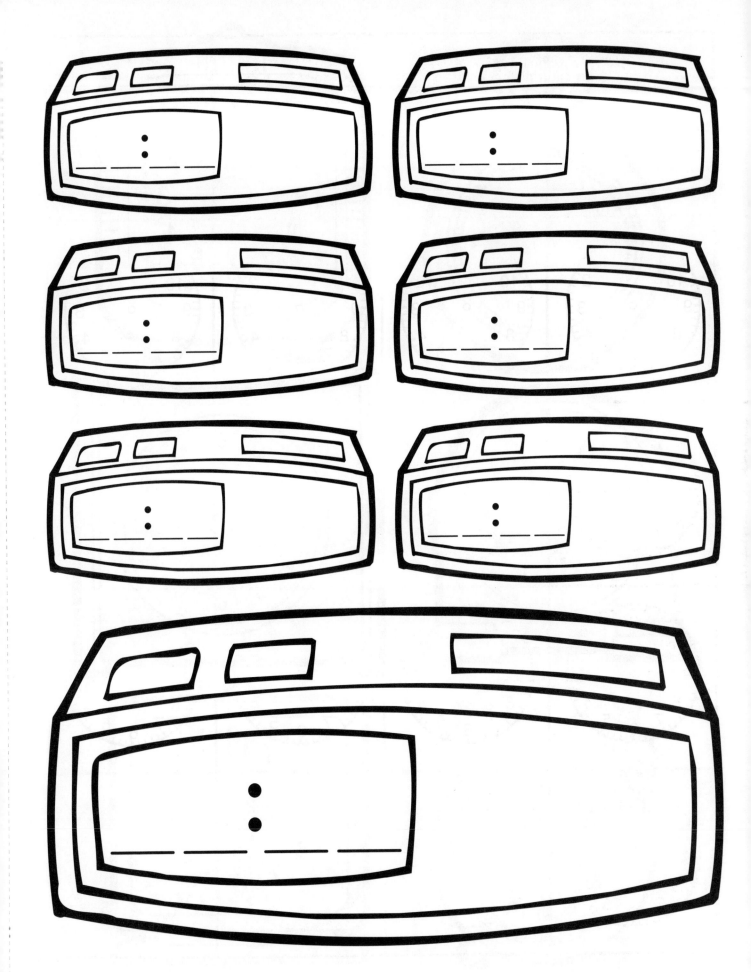

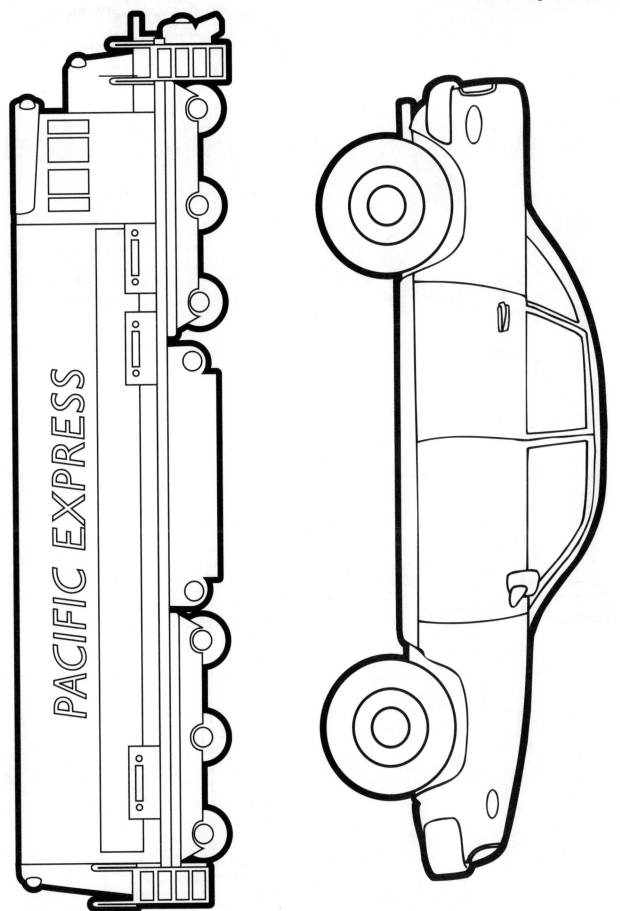

PACIFIC EXPRESS

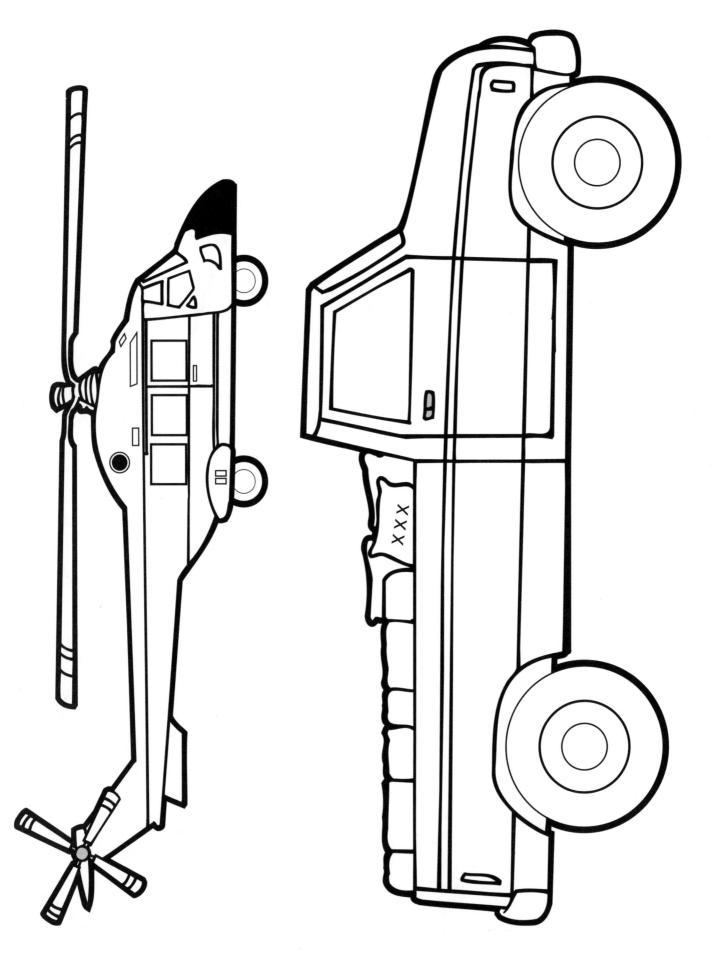

184 ©The Education Center, Inc. • *Big Book of Patterns* • TEC60802

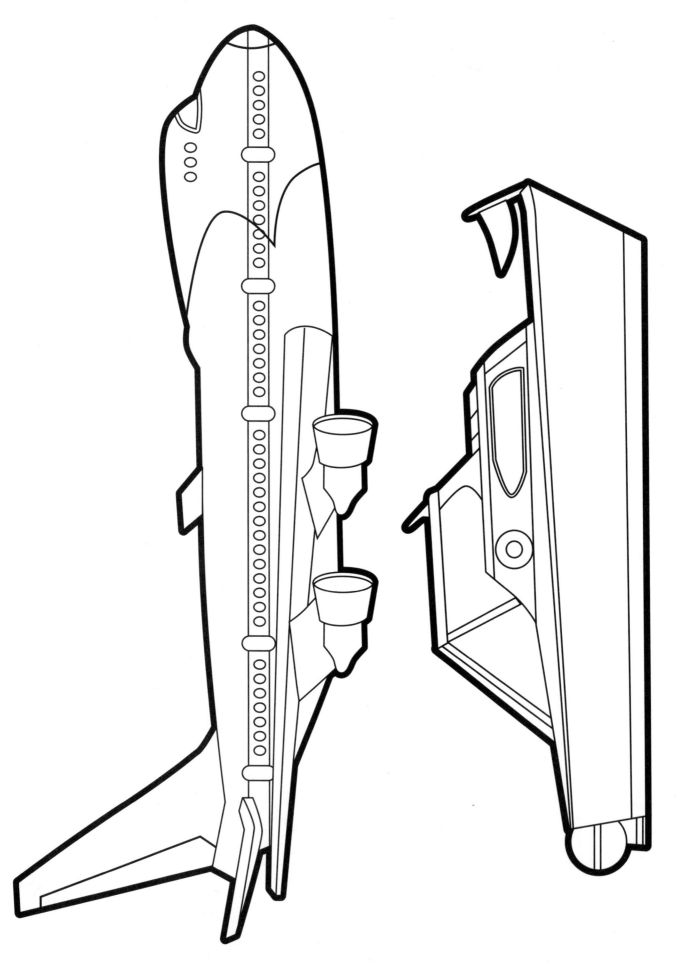

186 ©The Education Center, Inc. • *Big Book of Patterns* • TEC60802

188   ©The Education Center, Inc. • *Big Book of Patterns* • TEC60802

cloudy

rain

192

lightning

snow

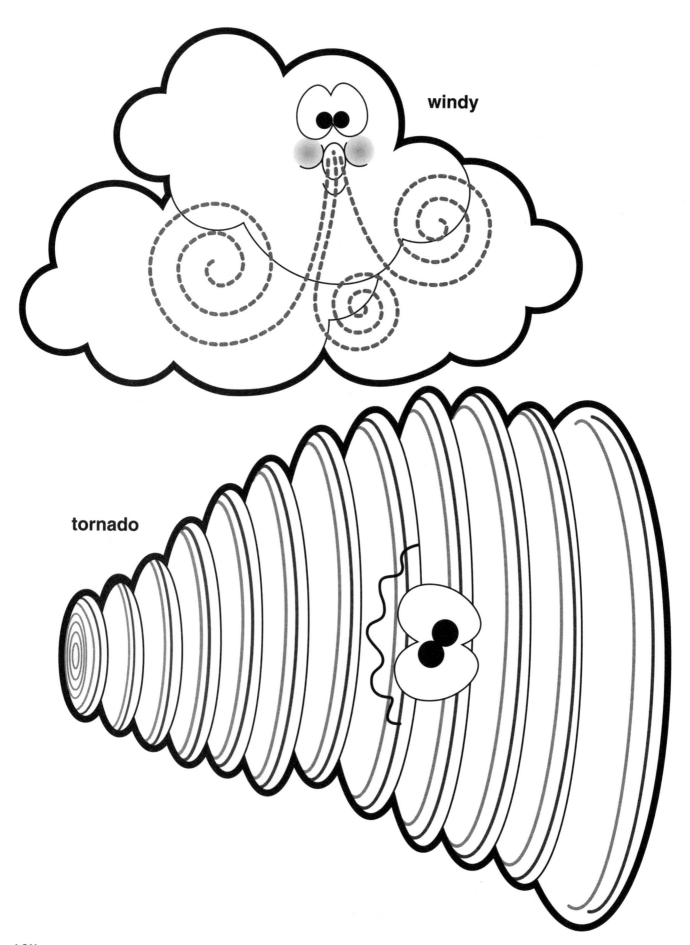

windy

tornado

194

1 CUP

3/4 CUP

1/2 CUP

1/4 CUP

1 TEASPOON

1 TEASPOON

1 CUP

VITAMIN D MILK 1/2 pint

VITAMIN D MILK 1 pint

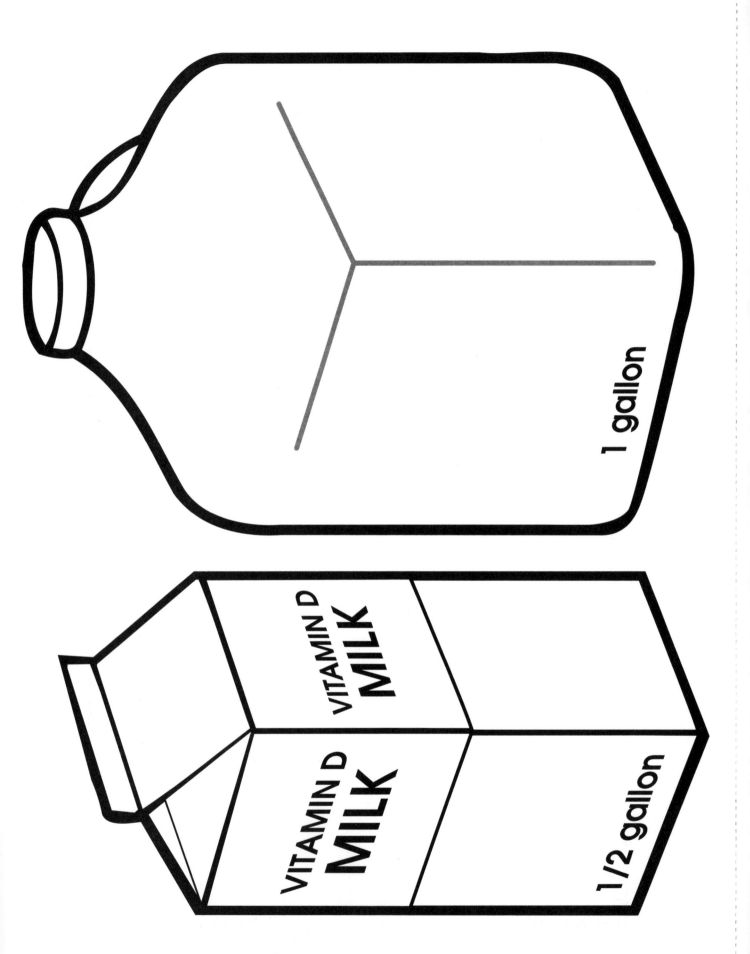

1 gallon

VITAMIN D
MILK

VITAMIN D
MILK

1/2 gallon

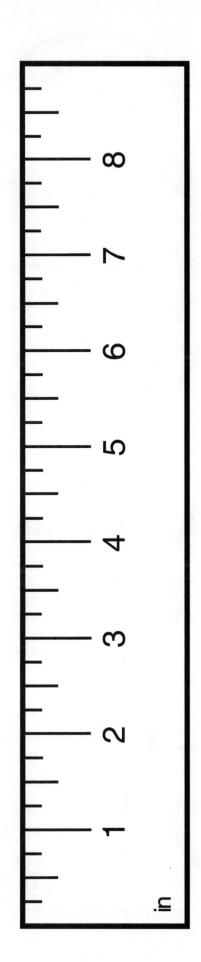

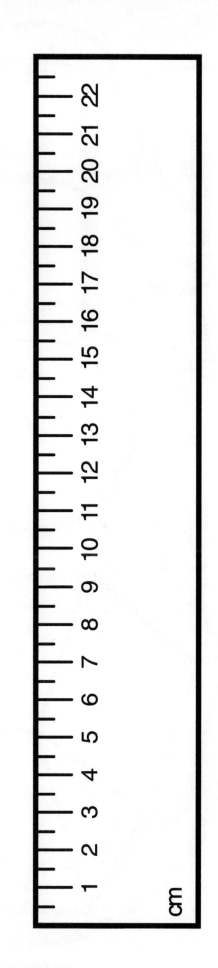

STEPS TO WRITING SUCCESS

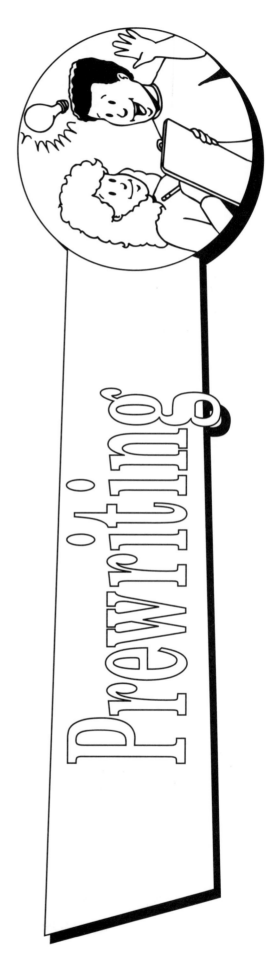

Prewriting

First Draft

Editing

DICTIONARY

Final Draft

Publishing